FAITH
BEYOND
LIP SERVICE

God's Model for Inclusion

La'Wana Harris

This book is dedicated to
followers of Jesus Christ.

Library of Congress Number- 2022922556
Print ISBN: 978-1-946388-25-4
Digital ISBN: 978-1-946388-30-8

Copyright 2023 by La'Wana Harris

All rights reserved. No part of this publication may be reproduced, distributed, or transmitted in any form or by any means, including photocopying, recording, or other electronic or mechanical methods, without the prior written permission of the author, except in the case of brief quotations embodied in critical reviews and certain other noncommercial uses permitted by copyright law. For permission requests, contact the author at info@lawanaharris.com.

Customization and Bulk sales: Special discounts are available on customizable bulk purchases by corporations, associations, and others. For details, contact the author at info@lawanaharris.com.

Printed in the United States of America

When it is available, we choose paper that has been manufactured by environmentally responsible processes. These may include using trees grown in sustainable forests, incorporating recycled paper, minimizing chlorine in bleaching, or recycling the energy produced at the paper mill.

CONTENTS

HOW TO USE THIS BOOK 4

INTRODUCTION: GOD'S HEART AND THE COMMIT FRAMEWORK 5

THE BIBLICAL CASE FOR DIVERSITY, EQUITY, AND INCLUSION

CHAPTER 1. MY STORY 15

CHAPTER 2. GOD'S HEART FOR DIVERSITY 22

CHAPTER 3. GOD'S HEART FOR INCLUSION 33

CHAPTER 4. THE DIVERSITY IN THE VERY EARLIEST CHURCH: THE TWELVE 52

CHAPTER 5. GOD'S HEART FOR LOVE 64

COMMIT TO A WAY FORWARD

CHAPTER 6. COMMIT TO COURAGEOUS ACTION (FOR FAMILY, CHURCH, THE WORLD) 76

CHAPTER 7. OPEN YOUR EYES AND EARS (TO THE GOOD, THE BAD, AND THE UGLY) 84

CHAPTER 8. MOVE BEYOND LIP SERVICE 94

CHAPTER 9. MAKE ROOM FOR CONTROVERSY AND CONFLICT 105

CHAPTER 10. INVITE NEW PERSPECTIVES 118

CHAPTER 11. TELL THE TRUTH EVEN WHEN IT HURTS 128

BIBLIOGRAPHY 144

HOW TO USE THIS BOOK

This book is part of my calling as a follower of Jesus Christ. Use it as a catalyst and a conversation starting point. The application will be the work that happens in your local congregation as you are engaging in the hard conversations that this book will bring up. It should be partnered with the Bible, teaching from the pulpit, and study in small groups. Use it for dinner conversations and the strengthening of relationships. Read it straight through, but then go back to the areas that challenge you most, and converse with each chapter in an honest way. The journey toward God's model for inclusion is a lifelong process that ends in Heaven. As the Kingdom of God is both already and not yet, so is our love for one another that crosses cultural lines. I wrote this with an open heart and mind, and my prayer is that you will read it in the same way.

INTRODUCTION: GOD'S HEART AND THE COMMIT FRAMEWORK

Diversity, equity, and inclusion (DEI) in the church have been elusive topics in many congregations despite the rise in global awareness. A pastor friend of mine told me that when he was planting a church in 2002, most of the church planters he knew were seeking to learn how to plant a healthy multiethnic church. The same pastor, a white man, told me that following the most recent civil unrest in the United States, his city divided, the nation divided, and his church divided. Issues that had lived lurking under the surface rose to the top and became too uncomfortable.

At that point, conversation fatigue had set in. People retreated to their comfort zones to rest up, tune out the Bible on the issue of DEI, and save the conversation for another day. But deep down, pastors like my friend had not forgotten the dream that God had given them two decades before. They had not forgotten the reasons they had prayed, worked, and fought for a unified and diverse church. They couldn't forget it because it was from God. It was biblical.

There are two biblical truths we hold in tension. The first is that God created us one human race.

> From one man he made all the nations, that they should inhabit the whole earth; and he marked out their appointed times in history and the boundaries of their lands (Acts 17:26 NIV).

As you go through your day, consider each person you meet as a soul to be introduced to Jesus Christ. Look at the person in the cubicle to your left, he is your brother. Look at the houseless woman who shouts profane curses at you when you walk by her sitting place, she is your sister. Look at that family going into that other church on Sundays where everyone looks like them, while you're on your way to the church where everyone looks like you—that's *your* family. We're all one race, the human race. We are all one family.

We hold this truth in tension with another:

> Come, let us go down and confuse their language so they will not understand each other. So the Lord scattered them from there over all the earth, and they stopped building the city. That is why it was called Babel—because there the Lord confused the language of the whole world. From there the Lord scattered them over the face of the whole earth (Gen 11:7-9 NIV).

This happened after the human race banded together to do something they thought was great. God had told them to spread across the world and populate it. They refused. But God wanted nations. He wanted Black people, white people, brown people … all fearfully and wonderfully made.

This birth of nation after nation meant the earth would get an abundance of cultures and customs. God created diversity as an integral part of his sovereign plan.

But because of sin, this would come with some baggage, some fear, and some hostility. It came with wars, slavery, genocides. It came with hatred, racism, phobias, scarcity, and pride.

Thankfully, God had mercy on his creation. Seeing that all this hate and evil came from the disobedience of one man, Adam, God came down and put his hand of blessing on a man, Abraham. From Abraham he would make a nation, and God would say,

> "… and through your offspring all nations on earth will be blessed, because you have obeyed me" (Gen 22:18 NIV).

What Abraham may not have understood was that from his seed, from the tribe of Judah would one day come the one who is both the Lion and the Lamb, born of a virgin to save the world and bring peace to *all men*. The Savior Jesus Christ would come to redeem the world.

He would not come to eradicate the nations and cultures but to unify them, starting with the demolition of a thick and tall wall of hostility between Abraham's old people and his new people.

> "For he himself is our peace, who has made the two groups one and has destroyed the barrier, the dividing wall of hostility" (Eph 2:14 NIV).

Consider how Christ called men and women from various nations at Pentecost, each one hearing the praises of God in his or her own language, reversing the confusion of Babel. Christ sent his disciples "to make disciples of all nations" (Mt 28:19). We are all called to discipleship in this generation.

To equip us for this great commission, Jesus gave us the power of love, the most disruptive idea the world has ever seen (and we are in need of a disruption). He gave us the ultimate truth, the power of forgiveness, and love for neighbor, brother, and even *enemies*. He gave us one baptism and a unifying Holy Spirit.

How have we stewarded these powerful gifts? We have not made the most of what we've been given. As a Church and the race of humanity, we have not done our part yet in the continuation of this restoration project as the hands and the feet of the one who saved us to be ambassadors of peace and reconciliation. We have not preached a gospel of peace with God and peace between the nations. We have not done what he left us here to do ... not yet.

I invite you to explore with me some of the reasons why this is true and how we might go about remedying this. We know everything we need to know for peace on earth and good will to men. But are we acting on what we know? My hope is that this book will help us to know and act.

My heart for this work can be illustrated by something that happened just as I was finishing this book. I am a committed follower of Jesus Christ. In my neighborhood, there is a gay couple who live across the street from me. I woke up to the chaos of sirens and the lights of police cars, fire trucks, and an ambulance. Realizing which house the first responders were at, I walked outside concerned for my neighbors. Other neighbors were outside watching, and some of us were praying while paramedics were inside the house. After some time, they emerged from the house with a body on a stretcher. His partner followed him out, distraught and with a heart-wrenching cry, announced to all of us, "he didn't make it."

Do you think I was thinking about a theological debate or political agenda? No, I was not. This fellow human, a fellow sojourner on the road of life in a fallen world, was in pain. The one he loved, his favorite person in the world, had perished. His life had just been shattered. I felt God's compassion, and I felt our shared humanity. My community is very conservative, but this was not a time for politics, theology, or debate. This was a human—hurting. And we all know what to do about that. This is what this book is about.

Faith Beyond Lip Service issues a clarion call to the body of Christ to live with eternity in mind. The Bible is clear about the diversity we will experience in eternity. People from every nation, tribe, and language will be in Heaven with God. Revelation 7:9–10 says:

> After this I looked, and behold, a great multitude that no one could number, from every nation, from all tribes and peoples and languages, standing before the throne and before the Lamb, clothed in white robes, with palm branches in their hands, and crying out with a loud voice, "Salvation belongs to our God who sits on the throne, and to the Lamb!" (ESV)

My posture in sharing this message is as a facilitator of a conversation that desperately needs to happen. I do not have a left, right, or middle agenda. I'm coming from a different space altogether that seeks to keep Jesus Christ at the center of our everyday interactions.

This book is about what we "do." It asks questions like: What specific actions do we take every day to honor God's model for inclusion? In Part 1, we will explore the biblical case for diversity, equity, and inclusion. In doing so, I'm inviting a deeper reliance on the love of God in Christ. God talks a lot more about diversity, equity, and inclusion than you might think. The Bible will be our reference point for discerning God's heart.

In Part 2, I'll introduce the tools for making change. The tools I will emphasize for operationalizing the principles in the book are found in what I call the COMMIT Inclusive Behavior Framework. Next, we will explore the fuel for the framework as followers of Jesus Christ—the Fruit of the Spirit (Gal 5:22–26).

After reading this book, I also created additional resources to continue the conversations and work in your local fellowship. *The Deed and Truth Journal* will help you continue your journey to Christ-centered DEI.

It's understandable that some believers are skeptical of messages related to diversity based on the prevalence of secular narratives centered around selfish ambitions. The current state of debate and deception does not negate the cause of Christ who came into the world to offer salvation to everyone. We must live and lead with that intention, and the local congregation should reflect that mindset. Embracing diversity, equity, and inclusion is a part of God's divine plan for all people to receive salvation—that none should perish.

According to the scriptures, everyone should be loved and welcomed into a caring body of believers. I invite you to move beyond words, beyond "lip service," to meaningful action that breaks the cycle of injustice and inequity that is often perpetrated in the body of Christ. We have an opportunity to not just ease into Heaven while the world goes to hell in a handbasket. We can COMMIT to being proactive in offering hope to our generation.

I invite you to COMMIT to greater intentionality and action for DEI grounded in the unconditional love of Christ. You likely already have an opinion about DEI, especially because it has garnered heightened awareness in almost every sphere of our culture, including the church. Maybe it has been a divisive topic in your church or around your dinner table. My goal is to pull the rug out from under the evil one's attempt to divide us before we even start the dialogue. I hope to define terms, to point out possible blind spots, to offer some meat to all "sides" of the "conversation." I will show that there is no argument unless we create one. I am a follower of Jesus Christ who is a Black woman and serves as a DEI strategist to churches and organizations. I've thought a lot about the intersection of the church and DEI (an understatement), and I long to be helpful and share what I've learned for the glory of God and the edification of the body of Christ.

In *Faith Beyond Lip Service*, I'm opening a dialogue with my fellow followers of Jesus Christ. What role do we play in honoring God's model for inclusion? What does the Bible say about diversity, equity, and inclusion? What clues can we decipher from God's creativity? How do we move forward in solidarity? What specific actions should we take to be the hands and feet of Christ?

Instead of being told at a traditional DEI training session that you need to be "more inclusive" and to make sure everyone can recite a DEI statement, *Faith Beyond Lip Service* supports you in developing your insights and corresponding actions about DEI from Christ's example.

There's no hidden agenda or propaganda—just love.

Looking "Godward" toward his plan for all nations to be gathered together in eternity, the COMMIT Inclusive Behavior Framework brings structure to Christ-centered DEI. Your conversations have a framework for building a mindset and environment where you can begin to model Christ's examples for inclusion during his earthly ministry. To COMMIT means to:

Commit to Courageous Action (for Family, Church, the World)

Open Your Eyes and Ears (to the Good, the Bad, and the Ugly)

Move Beyond Lip Service

Make Room for Controversy and Conflict

Invite New Perspectives

Tell the Truth Even When It Hurts

Although the inclusive behaviors sound (and are) simple, they are not necessarily easy.

We will also explore the Fruit of the Spirit as practical principles to put our commitment into action to be salt and light to this generation.

PART One:

THE BIBLICAL CASE FOR DIVERSITY, EQUITY, AND INCLUSION

CHAPTER ONE:
My Story

My story is a complicated and messy saga about a little girl and her big God. I'm one of those people that still believes one person can change the world by focusing on helping one soul at a time.

Although I believe in the power of helping one person at a time, writing this book (something that has the potential to help a lot of people at once) is an integral part of my Christian calling at this phase of my life.

Most people would refer to this stage as *retirement*. I refer to it as the time where the balance of my "get to's" and "got to's" has shifted. I am now at the place where I spend the majority of my time focusing on activities and things that I "get to" do. This is a blessing—and a responsibility.

The funny thing about this book is that it is a "got to." I feel compelled to start this conversation while staying in my lane as a born again, spirit-filled believer. My hope is that pastors, teachers, and small group leaders will take the conversations that begin in this book and continue this important work in their congregations.

Writing from this point of clarity keeps me focused on my two simple goals:

1. To offer a Christ-centered approach for diversity, equity, and inclusion
2. To provide support and tools that edify the body of Christ and give glory to God

I said there are some "messy" aspects of my story. I have never truly fit into anyone's box for how people generally categorize and identify themselves. For example, I am a Black woman, and most people interact with me based on what they see. This means that people tend to assume things about me that align to the narrative of these two aspects of my identity—being Black and being a woman. If you saw my picture when you picked up this book on DEI, then you likely assumed some things too.

However, the most important aspect of my identity is not my race or my gender, but rather, it is my *faith*. My relationship with Jesus Christ trumps any other aspect of my lived experience. Working and living as a believer in secular spaces has created some messy situations and shaped who I am and how I think.

Most notably, my life is full of realities that people call contradictions but really aren't. They say, for instance, that Bibles and guns, two prominent features of my Southern upbringing, cannot coexist along with my peaceful protesting from my lived experience as a Black woman. This clash of reality, ideology, and expectations has shown up repeatedly as a prominent feature of both my personal and professional life.

For example, I was recently ridiculed on a Zoom call by a professional peer for drinking from a Chick-fil-A cup. Why? Because they assumed as a Black woman, I am marginalized enough to know that Chick-fil-A is not progressive. But don't worry, I have faced opposition from the right as well. I've had Christian friends chastise me for my unconditional love for my son after he came out as queer.

This messiness even appeared in the process of writing this book. It was hard finding editorial and publishing support from those who were able to put their personal preferences aside and remain objective about the intersection of faith and DEI. This tells me this book is desperately needed. I am not at the center of the left and the right but in another space entirely, and I believe I am there with Jesus.

So, if despite my best efforts, you feel that you are discerning an agenda as you read this, please charge it to my head and not my heart because having an agenda is not the intention at all. I'm bringing all my experiences, expertise, successes, and failures into this space with you as a fellow believer.

Foundational Principles

As a form of introduction, I'd like to share a couple foundational principles that guide my life as I share part of my story. I've already alluded to one—God first. While I readily admit that I make mistakes every day, my sincerest goal is to try to keep God first in everything I do and please him above all. But despite my best efforts, sometimes I still miss the mark and need grace from God and people—*we all do.*

The second foundational principle I'd like to share comes from my life purpose statement: "I'm called to live my life as a distribution center, not a storage facility."

I remember hearing this phrase in my spirit during a time of prayer as I was seeking God about the purpose for my life. Shortly after hearing this phrase and writing it in my prayer journal, I saw a vision of myself with my right hand extended up to the sky and my left hand extended out in front of me. God let me know that he would pour blessings through me to the world.

That prayer experience happened more than three decades ago, and I am still receiving new revelation about how I'm called to serve as a follower of Jesus Christ. I imagine that I will until Jesus returns or calls me home. I've learned to not get attached to anything that comes into my life because at any moment God may ask me to give it away to someone in need, to *distribute it from him through me.*

I know this concept may seem strange in this "it's all about me" and "living my best life" generation. But it's true. Ask anyone in my immediate family and they will tell you, "Goodwill is La'Wana's favorite place to shop."

Career Path

After growing up in a Christian home in the South, I went to community college and got my associate degree in radiology before going on to get my bachelor's degree in biology 10 years and three children later.

The original plan was that I would become a physician and serve as a missionary in Darfur, South Sudan. But love had other plans. My boyfriend at the time and I decided to get married shortly after finishing high school. I'm happy to say he's still my boyfriend after 33 years of marriage.

Following the path of most newlyweds, we started our family and entered what I call our struggle years. My husband worked in construction, and I worked as a medical assistant, mobile mammographer, and radiologic technologist. It was truly the best of times and the worst of times—but we survived by God's grace.

Years later, I worked as a floating nurse while finishing my bachelor's degree. Pharmaceutical sales representatives and their managers would frequently visit the offices. They would always tell me they loved my personality and thought I would be great in their industry. Eventually, they convinced me to take a deeper look at the opportunity as it began to sink in that medical school was less and less a viable option for a mom in a struggling family with three small children.

Looking back on that transition, I jokingly say, "I went over to the dark side." The truth is that I'm grateful for the blessings afforded to my family from the years spent in the pharmaceutical industry. I was able to travel the world, lead, coach, and develop scores of professionals while lifting my family out of poverty.

Since leaving my last position in the corporate world, director of global leadership development, I've retired to a 55+ golf community in Florida. I still do some consulting and serve as a member of the adjunct faculty at the University of Pennsylvania in the Organizational Dynamics program. Though I like being retired, I think I'll always try to do "a little something" as long as I'm able to do so. I've always loved being productive—especially for the Kingdom of God.

As part of my corporate career, I also became a certified diversity executive, an International Coach Federation (ICF) accredited coach, and a global DEI strategist, and I now have decades of professional experience in those spheres. My great hope is to use all my expertise to bring about meaningful change in the body of Christ.

While working in the corporate world, I also felt called into various ministries. From missions in Haiti to children's ministry to being a Rapid Response Chaplain and serving in street evangelism and outreach, I have experienced a broad range of being the hands and feet of Jesus in his work. My goal is to use up every ounce of my God-given talent before he calls me home, so at any point in time, I have two or three major projects going, especially as I feel God's pull to pass on what I've learned to the next generation to add value in these trying times.

What Box Am I In?

Finally, let's address the box that a lot of people want me to check. Am I right, left, or middle?

My answer is and will always be—*none of the above*. I get it. So many people, especially in my generation, are completely consumed with the answer to that question. I'm sorry, but I'm not one of them. I heard a term that resonates best with me from Pastor Rod Parsley, "I'm a Christ-o-crat."

Honestly, I'm most concerned with the box, if we stick with that metaphor, that I can check indicating I am *redeemed*. My focus is on the box that indicates my name is written in the

Lamb's Book of Life (Rev 13:8). It's not popular thinking, but my priorities are different from the mainstream narrative. Go ahead and assume you know what it means. You'll be wrong. I don't fit in any box but his.

So, this book will not serve any political agenda. My official statement is that I try to make decisions based on my dedication to my values and beliefs according to my faith as a follower of Jesus Christ. And as Forrest Gump says, "That's all I have to say about that."

What this book *will* do is challenge you, no matter which side you've taken, to consider why you've taken a *side*. Why not look at each issue under the Word of God and the influence of the Holy Spirit? Why not forget what you've been told by the media and the culture warriors who profit off your outrage and look with me to the Bible, to the truth? That's my challenge, and if you accept, turn (or scroll) the page.

CHAPTER TWO:

God's Heart for Diversity

Some believe that Christianity is at odds with DEI. But it isn't. "Diversity," according to the *Merriam-Webster Dictionary*, is "the state of having people of different races or who have different cultures in a group or organization."

While that is one definition, the idea of diversity stretches far past race and culture. Anything that makes us different from one another is part of what it means to be diverse. At one time, America was legally segregated by evil laws put in place to ensure a lack of diversity, equity, and inclusion. Dr. Martin Luther King Jr was one of the pioneers who helped change all that.

Dr. King once said that Sunday was the most homogenous day of the week. Sadly, since his time, not much has changed. Most churches you visit still have clusters of the same kinds of people in their pews. In your average church service, you are not seeing the beautiful diversity of God's creation.

However, in recent years, there has been more conversation about embracing diversity in the church. Many Christians want to engage deeper in discipleship and understanding of people from all walks of life, but they don't know how. A great place to start is to honor God and his plan for creation and humanity. After all, God created all the diversity we see today, so in celebrating it, we are celebrating him.

In his book, *The Big Sort*, Bill Bishop notes something interesting. He argues that although America has become increasingly diverse, the places where we live are fraught with people who live, think, and vote like us. In other words, Americans tend to be homogenous creatures living in like-minded communities within a diverse culture. Sadly, we often still see this in churches as well, despite the incremental progress that has been made.

In fact, [1]Lifeway Research found that 53 percent of churchgoers disagreed with the following statement: "My church needs to become more ethnically diverse." In other words, most believers are comfortable with the level (or lack) of diversity in their church. At least part of them fears how things would change if their church became more diverse. As a result, there are Christians who oppose and intentionally neglect diversity. While diverse, multicultural, multiethnic, multiracial, and multigenerational churches exist, there are relatively few of them.

In addition to this statistic, only 20 percent of pastors and staff report even speaking about racial reconciliation and diversity. These two stats are very disappointing. But the current

---

1   Postell, M. (2022, January 24). The Group Most Likely to Still Be Missing From Your Church. Insights. https://research.lifeway.com/2022/01/24/the-group-most-likely-to-still-be-missing-from-your-church/

evangelical and cultural environment lends itself to the church embracing action on this issue.

The truth is God is creating a people (singular) for himself from all peoples (plural)—people from every tribe, nation, tongue, and group (Rev. 7:9; 5:9). Therefore, the beauty of Heaven should be reflected in the diversity of the church. Multiethnic churches are a preview of God's eternal Kingdom. Furthermore, they are a sign from God. Jesus said, "they will know that you are my disciples, if you love one another" (Jn 13:35).

We know—historically and currently—this is not easy. But the difficulty of diversity should not stop us from working toward more diverse churches, especially if it means we can correct Satan's lies and bring truth through the conversation.

Consider the diversity within the Godhead itself. We speak of God as Trinity: Father, Son, and Holy Spirit. We believe that these three are distinct persons made of one essence who work in perfect unity and harmony with one another. The beauty of this is in the unity that is found even in their diversity: Father, Son, and Holy Spirit work toward the same goals in unity and love for one another. Nothing could ever divide them.

God's Image-Bearers

Recall now that we are made in God's image. That means that the diversity found in the world, especially in humanity, reflects the diversity that's found within the Godhead itself. Therefore, when we work in harmony with the diversity of the human race, each taking our own experiences, backgrounds, and callings to further the work of God's Kingdom, we reflect God's heart and character.

Diversity is what makes us God's very nature and character. The unity expressed through the Holy Trinity is the very definition of love. It's precisely why the Bible tells us that "God is love" (1 Jn 4:8). Their love binds them together as one: God our loving Father in Heaven, Jesus our Lord and Savior, and the Holy Spirit our helper within us.

Diverse Genders

A beautiful way to look at the diverse yet divinely designed nature of the two genders is in the bringing forth of children. Let's look at Genesis 1:26–27.

> Then God said, "Let us make mankind in our image, in our likeness, so that they may rule over the fish in the sea and the birds in the sky, over the livestock and all the wild animals, and over all the creatures that move along the ground."
> God created mankind in his own image, in the image of God he created them; male and female he created them (NIV).

This may seem like a simple passage at first glance, but there is much to uncover just beneath the surface. First, God said, "Let us make mankind in our image." God is three in one. He is Father, Son, and Holy Spirit. Humanity came forth from the diversity of these three who are one. Their unity in diversity is what brought us into this world in the first place.

God created the diversity within the human race. We are each created in his image for his pleasure and glory (Revelation 4:11; Colossians 1:16). He designed us the way we are and delights in his handiwork (Psalm 139:13–16).

God calls us to treat everyone with the same love and respect that Jesus Himself displayed toward us, even going as far as to endure death on the cross on our behalf.

Romans 2:11 says, "For there is no respect of persons with God" (KJV). This verse tells us that God does not show favoritism. That means that any kind of racism has no place in our hearts. We must never believe that God would love or accept us more than he would anyone else in this world. Unfortunately, many have fallen into that trap, which does not lead to a godly life.

God's love is all-consuming, unconditional, and available to all. There is nothing that disqualifies us from the love of God. Remember that Jesus loved everyone. He ministered to those considered by society to be holy and those considered to be sinners. He did this because He knew that God loves them the same. He wanted them all to have the same access to the healing and restorative power of God's love.

Romans 8:38–39 captures this truth brilliantly:

> And I am convinced that nothing can ever separate us from God's love. Neither death nor life, neither angels nor demons, neither our fears for today nor our worries about tomorrow—not even the powers of hell can separate us from God's love. No power in the sky above or in the earth below—indeed, nothing in all creation will ever be able to separate us from the love of God that is revealed in Christ Jesus our Lord (NLT).

What does this truth reveal to us about diversity? If we follow God's ways, we must never believe that anyone is outside of God's love. Instead, we must treat them with the same love, dignity, and respect that Jesus showed to all. He must be our prime example in everything.

We are all the children of God and are called to join together as a family of faith. Let's pray that God's love binds us together with cords that cannot be broken. When we live in that way, we will see the differences between us as a blessing from the Lord.

Diversity of Gifts

Our unity in diversity creates great outcomes for the cause of God's Kingdom. We are all given unique and special spiritual gifts distributed by the Holy Spirit. These are given according to God's design for us from which he created us in the womb. 1 Corinthians 12:12-14 says:

> Just as a body, though one, has many parts, but all its many parts form one body, so it is with Christ. For we were all baptized by one Spirit so as to form one body—whether Jews or Gentiles, slave or free—and we were all given the one Spirit to drink. Even so the body is not made up of one part but of many (NIV).

Together, we make up the body of Christ. When people come together and bring with them their race, culture, background, experiences, and gifts we can accomplish miraculous things together for God's Kingdom.

The Disciples Were Diverse

This truth is seen clearly in the story of the disciples. There were people of all backgrounds and experiences joining Jesus' inner circle. Matthew provides one of the most striking examples of all. He was a Jew who worked for the Romans as a tax collector. As a result, he was hated by his people. In those times, tax collectors were seen as the worst of the worst. Why? Because they were notorious for taking the money of the repressed Jewish people and giving it to the cruel and greedy Romans. They were also often accused of taking extra to line their pockets.

What made Matthew's situation even worse was the fact that he was a Jew himself. That made him despised among his people. For many Jews, it was bad enough that the Romans were oppressing them and taking their money in taxes, but it was even worse that one of their own people was working for the Romans and helping them in this task. They felt it was a betrayal of the highest order.

Could you imagine the horror of the other disciples when Jesus called Matthew to follow Him? They must have second-guessed him, maybe even wondered if he had made a mistake. But Jesus was trying to get the point across that all are called by God. Moreover, all are welcomed into Jesus' inner circle by answering the call to salvation and a life of Christian service. God loves everyone, both the most pious people and the tax collectors.

Diversity Is Biblical

As I previously quoted, God created mankind and gave it some orders. God intended from the beginning that men and women would not only represent God on earth as delegated authorities, but they were to *multiply*. Not only were they to multiply, but they were to cover the face of the earth. In short, they were to become many nations.

After blessing them, God commanded them to fill the earth, to have dominion over every living thing *on the earth*. They needed to spread out. In short, God's desire was for nations. Later, he repeated this command to Noah and his family. "And God blessed Noah and his sons and said to them, 'Be fruitful and multiply and fill the earth'" (Gen 9:1 ESV).

Instead, they decided they'd rather stay put. Humanity, after a few generations, had their own ideas. They'd build one great big city. One big global capital so everyone could be the same. They would build a monument of a tower as a token of their greatness. God looked and realized that the human desire for homogeneity was a problem and was causing them to disobey his command to make nations all over the world (Gen 11).

Now the Lord said to Abram:

> Go from your country and your kindred and your father's house to the land that I will show you. And I will make of you a great nation, and I will bless you and make your name great, so that you will be a blessing. I will bless those who bless you, and him who dishonors you I will curse, and in you all the families of the earth shall be blessed (Gen 12:1–3 ESV).

Fast-forward to the ministry of Jesus. He commissions the disciples (and his Church) to the nations.

And Jesus came and said to them, "All authority in heaven and on earth has been given to me. Go therefore and make disciples of all nations, baptizing them in the name of the Father and of the Son and of the Holy Spirit, teaching them to observe all that I have commanded you. And behold, I am with you always, to the end of the age" (Mat 28:18–20 ESV).

Then in Acts 1, Luke says that Jesus' last words to his disciples on earth after the resurrection were:

> It is not for you to know times or seasons that the Father has fixed by his own authority. But you will receive power when the Holy Spirit has come upon you, and you will be my witnesses in Jerusalem and in all Judea and Samaria, and to **the end of the earth** (Acts 1:7–8 ESV, emphasis added).

The apostle Paul gives us one of the most compelling examples of biblical diversity by addressing the issue found in his letter to the Ephesian Church and his great and powerful explanation of the demolishing of the ancient wall of hostility between Jews and Gentiles in their day. We will look more closely at this in later chapters, as well as the evidence from Revelation that God will preserve the uniqueness of the nations in the new heavens and new earth to come following the second coming of Christ, the King of Kings of the Nations.

Diversity Is Humble

The Jews in the Bible struggled with ethnocentrism, believing they were better or superior to Gentiles. They knew they were the chosen people, and they looked down on the ways of the Gentiles. Compounding the complexity of the issue was that they were subject to the Gentiles in the time of Christ. But God did not want them to consider themselves superior. And he did not want them to consider the Gentiles beyond salvation.

The Gentiles also looked down on the Jews, as had other groups in the past, such as the Egyptians. For example, when Joseph's family came to Egypt, they could not eat with Joseph because they were Jews and shepherds. Eventually, they would be enslaved by the Pharaohs.

Some people continue to struggle in our day with the balance of celebrating who they are and feeling superior to others. However, if we are to establish inclusive environments that foster Christ-centered diversity, many people will have to forgo their pride. It requires us to be willing to include, follow, and learn from people with very different experiences and backgrounds.

[2]Charles Spurgeon says, "There is nothing the human heart falls into as easily as pride, and yet there is no sin that is more frequently, more emphatically, and more eloquently condemned in Scripture. Pride is unjustified." Diversity is humble.

Diversity Is Intentional

We must be intentional if we want diversity that honors God's plan. We must constantly cast a vision for God's heart for diversity and take action to inspire participation by diverse people.

---

2   Spurgeon, C. (2019, November 30). Faithful to Christ: A Challenge to Truly Live for Christ [Quote]. Aneko Press.

One of the main goals of this book is to encourage this intentionality and offer practical tools for next steps once that decision is made. 1 Corinthians 9:24–26 says:

> Do you not know that in a race all the runners run, but only one receives the prize? So run that you may obtain it. Every athlete exercises self-control in all things. They do it to receive a perishable wreath, but we an imperishable. So I do not run aimlessly; I do not box as one beating the air (ESV).

Paul understood that "running aimlessly" or "beating the air" would not get him the prize. Assuming our prize is a church that looks like Heaven in its diversity, we must aim our punches and run to win. We must decide that diversity is worth it for effective evangelism and discipleship.

Diversity Is Beneficial

Deciding that diversity is worth it starts with understanding that diversity is beneficial. Diversity in the church benefits the whole church. Diversity broadens our perspectives, understanding, and even our application of Scripture.

Most Christians simply do not leave their comfortable bubbles. They may be comfortable, but they are missing much of the richness of the Holy Spirit's work through other kinds of people and churches who are still destined to live together with them in eternity, worshiping the Lamb of God. Simply put, God created and then saved those people who are different from you, and he has a purpose through them that goes beyond just reaching people in their own group.

CHAPTER THREE:

God's Heart for Inclusion

When the day of Pentecost arrived, **they were all together in one place**. And suddenly there came from heaven a sound like a mighty rushing wind, and it filled the entire house where they were sitting. And divided tongues as of fire appeared to them and rested on each one of them. And they were **all filled with the Holy Spirit** and began to speak in **other tongues** as the Spirit gave them utterance.

Now there were **dwelling in Jerusalem Jews, devout men from every nation under heaven**. And at this sound **the multitude came together**, and they were bewildered, because **each one was hearing them speak in his own language**. And they were amazed and astonished, saying, "Are not all these who are speaking Galileans? And how is it that **we hear, each of us in his own native language**? Parthians and Medes and Elamites and residents of Mesopotamia, Judea and Cappadocia, Pontus and Asia, Phrygia and Pamphylia, Egypt and the parts of Libya belonging to Cyrene, and visitors from Rome, both Jews and proselytes, Cretans and Arabians—we hear them **telling in our own tongues the mighty works of God**." And all were **amazed and perplexed**, saying to one another, "What does this mean?" But **others mocking** said, "They are filled with new wine." (Acts 2:1–13 ESV, emphasis added)

There's no doubt about it: God gives explicit examples for us to follow his heart for inclusion. This passage alone makes that crystal clear. Just look at some of the bold text:

- They were all together in one place
- All filled with the Holy Spirit
- Other tongues
- Dwelling in Jerusalem … devout men from every nation under heaven
- We hear, each of us in his own native language

We also, sadly, get a glimpse of why diversity and inclusion are so difficult. Many were perplexed, and some were even mocking God's plan for inclusion.

Diversity refers to having people with differences in the same group. Inclusion means not just having them but having them as an integral part, giving them a place at the table, such as God has done in his salvation of the nations.

Arguably the most well-known verse in the entire Bible is John 3:16. In John chapter 3, Nicodemus, a Pharisee and member of the ruling religious class, comes to visit Jesus in the night away from the accusing eyes of his fellow Pharisees. Even though his brethren don't believe in Jesus and his teachings, Nicodemus does believe and wants to learn more from Jesus.

Nicodemus affirms his faith that Jesus was a wise teacher who came from God Himself. Then Jesus begins to explain the heart of the Gospel message, that one must be "born again" to enter the Kingdom of God. Nicodemus asks how one could be born again once they have already come out from their mother's womb. Jesus explains how it is a spiritual rebirth and not a physical one. He then goes on to say,

> "For God so loved the world, that he gave his only Son, that whoever believes in him should not perish but have eternal life."

Jesus did not say that God gave His only Son so that a specific people, group, or particular background could receive eternal life. Instead, Jesus said anyone who calls on the name of Jesus could receive salvation.

I must ask this question: If Jesus uses such *inclusive language* and doesn't deny anyone access to salvation, why would we? It's shocking, sad, and downright frustrating to hear stories of churches and believers who shun others or do not let them participate in their church's community for any reason. That is not our place. No matter who someone is, where they are from, or what they have done, God can and will work on their hearts. If we deny them fellowship or Christian love, we are doing an injustice to them and God Himself.

In Matthew 25, Jesus talks about the day of judgment when He will separate those who believe and put their faith in him versus those who don't.

When the Son of Man comes in his glory, and all the angels with him, then he will sit on his glorious throne. Before him will be gathered all the nations, and he will separate people one from another as a shepherd separates the sheep from the goats. And he will place the sheep on his right, but the goats on the left. Then the King will say to those on his right, "Come, you who are blessed by my Father, inherit the kingdom prepared for you from the foundation of the world. For I was hungry and you gave me food, I was thirsty and you gave me drink, I was a stranger and you welcomed me, I was naked and you clothed me, I was sick and you visited me, I was in prison and you came to me." Then the righteous will answer him, saying, "Lord, when did we see you hungry and feed you, or thirsty and give you drink? And when did we see you a stranger and welcome you, or naked and clothe you? And when did we see you sick or in prison and visit you?" And the King will answer them, "Truly, I say to you, as you did it to one of the least of these my brothers, you did it to me."

> Then he will say to those on his left, "Depart from me, you cursed, into the eternal fire prepared for the devil and his angels. For I was hungry and you gave me no food, I was thirsty and you gave me no drink, I was a stranger and you did not welcome me, naked and you did not clothe me, sick and in prison and you did not visit me." Then they also will answer, saying, "Lord, when did we see you hungry or thirsty or a stranger or naked or sick or in prison, and did not minister to you?" Then he will answer them, saying, "Truly, I say to you, as you did not do it to one of the least of these, you did not do it to me." And these will go away into eternal punishment, but the righteous into eternal life. (Mt 25:31–46 ESV).

In this passage, Jesus mentions a wide array of people: those who are hungry, strangers that need clothes, those who are sick, and those who find themselves in prison. In these verses, Jesus calls us to love and minister to all these types of people and more.

He says that those who have loved, served, and ministered to these individuals will receive salvation. They are the true believers. Jesus says he will welcome them into eternity with him at the end times. But those who shun these people and do not show them the love of Christ are in trouble. They are not living out true faith in Christ, and the fruits of their lives have shown it.

In Matthew 25:45–46, Jesus has these words for those people:

> "'Truly I tell you, whatever you did not do for one of the least of these, you did not do for me.' And these will go away into eternal punishment, but the righteous to eternal life" (NIV).

Jesus' message is clear: he does not welcome those who do not welcome others. We must take His words seriously.

Just look at the beautiful words of Paul written in his book to the Galatians in chapter 3 verse 28:

> "There is neither Jew nor Greek, there is neither slave nor free, there is no male and female, for you are all one in Christ Jesus."

An extraordinary change happens once we accept Christ into our hearts. *All the labels and all the ways we once defined ourselves are gone.* We are now children of God above everything. We all have equal standing under our common Father in Heaven. He loves us all equally and unconditionally, giving us all a common purpose to fulfill.

While it is true that God chose the Jews and they will always have a special place, God doesn't claim one people as his own. God doesn't subscribe to any specific political agenda. God doesn't want us to bicker over secular issues. He desires that we would love as He loves. We should welcome all into his glorious and eternal Kingdom with an invitation to receive Jesus Christ as their Lord and Savior.

Paul showed us a heart for inclusion when he wrote to the Romans. Romans 12:15–18 says,

> "Rejoice with those who rejoice, weep with those who weep. Live in harmony with one another. Do not be haughty, but associate with the lowly. Never be wise in your own sight. Repay no one evil for evil, but give thought to do what is honorable in the sight of all. If possible, so far as it depends on you, live peaceably with all."

There is much to unpack here.

First, we're called to *rejoice with those who rejoice*. Life is full of joy and blessings from God. He loves us as his children and treats us with the care of a loving Father. He seeks our best interests, guides us through life, and gives us gifts only he can give. Rejoicing with those who are celebrating God's blessings is a joy for them and us. Likewise, celebrating with others is an excellent relationship builder. Consider for a moment the most intimate relationships in your life. How were those relationships built? They were built on the memories you have together. Many of these memories are likely of celebrating joyous occasions together. Joy is contagious, and God wishes that we'd share it with our brothers and sisters in Christ.

But this verse also tells us to *weep with those who weep*. Great relationships are also built by mutual grieving. When those we love are hurting, sad, or disappointed, we should share in their pain with them. It helps to know that a brother or sister in Christ has their back and is there to comfort them. Those moments can help build relationships just as much, if not more so, than the joyous moments. Enduring trials alongside one another helps to build bonds that last a lifetime. John 13:34 says,

> "A new commandment I give to you, that you love one another: just as I have loved you, you also are to love one another."

This whole book is about love, but we'll talk more about love specifically in Chapter 5.

Next, we are told to *live in harmony with one another*. How? By what follows:

> ...Do not be haughty, but associate with the lowly. Never be wise in your own sight. Repay no one evil for evil, but give thought to do what is honorable in the sight of all. If possible, so far as it depends on you, live peaceably with all.
> (Romans 12:16–18 ESV)

Harmony with others comes as a result of:

Not being haughty—Pride kills. God hates it because it gets in the way of living a godly life. When one is haughty, he looks down on others. Living in harmony is not possible when our haughtiness causes us to think of ourselves more highly than we should.

Associating with the lowly—Do you associate with the lowly? Do you believe that faith in Christ is truly an equalizer of persons? Do you believe that your relationships, especially in the church, are to be based on the shared Holy Spirit in you and the brother or sister you see as lowly? Reflect on the difference between those Jesus will categorize as sheep and goats. Those who associate with the lowly have understood that Christ dwells in the lowly. Step one is to go where the lowly are and be with them. Serve them in a way that doesn't put you on a higher level. Don't serve in a way that creates an "Us vs. Them" mentality in either one of you. Look for ways to create reciprocal relationships with those the culture would say are "beneath you."

Then step two is to simply train yourself to see as God sees. All of us are lowly to God, yet he accepts us as his beloved children. Ask the Lord to help you, and he will.

Never being wise in your own sight—This is similar to pride, but it is specifically pride of knowledge and wisdom. You may think you are smarter and wiser than those you would like to exclude. In the next chapter, we will discuss the homogeneous church. In these churches, which are the majority of local churches, people flock together with people like themselves. There is absolutely nothing impressive about that from the perspective of love. Any type of organization can build around homogeneity. We are psychologically wired for it.

Repay no one evil for evil, but give thought to do what is honorable in the sight of all—This is the heart of the Gospel and the centerpiece of Christian faith. It's also the starting point for inclusion. Jesus calls us to love everyone, even our enemies. To know who we are in Christ is to have a deep sense of security in him and, as a result, in ourselves.

The natural man cannot return blessing for evil because he is threatened, his sense of himself, that is, his identity and self-esteem, is threatened. The Christian is not natural but supernatural. He or she begins with identity in Christ. We know that God has accepted us, redeemed us, and given us his name, his identity, and all the "perks" that go with it, namely a great inheritance and a house with him in Heaven.

We start there, fully accepted, and we live according to his ways, stewards of the life and talents he has given us, enjoying our life in him and accomplishing the purposes for the work he has called us to. If you are not working for God's purposes, make it a priority to seek him and know what he has made and called you to do.

When Jesus is your identity, you have nothing to lose by forgiving others. You have new wisdom, and you can be like your Father who "causes his sun to rise on the evil and the good" (Mt 5:45 NIV). It does you no harm to love your enemies. It actually helps you. When you can walk in your identity in Christ and refuse to repay evil for evil, you can be a mighty force for inclusion, avoiding the traps and conflicts that the evil one likes to use when people from different cultures come together.

If possible, so far as it depends on you, live peaceably with all. This is a self-evident statement. When there is a conflict, when there is a possibility of *not* living peaceably with all, look to this command. God says, "if possible, live peaceably with all." It is true that sometimes it does not "depend on you." You often cannot do anything about it when someone else is bent on aggression toward you, but there are times when it does depend on you. Don't escalate. Remember that your identity in Christ gives you grounds to forgive. Be like your Lord who said, bleeding and suffocating on a Roman cross, "Father, forgive them, for they do not know what they are doing" (Lk 23:34 NIV).

Equity and Bias

Equity means to be fair or impartial. God shows equity toward all his creation. God doesn't play favorites or show partiality toward one group of people as opposed to another. Whoever claims this to be true is mistaken. God created everyone and loves us all the same.

There are many examples of God's equity:

- Isaiah 11:4 says:

> But with righteousness shall he judge the poor, and reprove with equity for the meek of the earth: and he shall smite the earth with the rod of his mouth, and with the breath of his lips shall he slay the wicked. (KJV)

In this verse, we see that God's focus and concern is on how we live our lives and not anything to do with our background, race, or anything else.

- Romans 2:11 says,

> "For God shows no partiality" (ESV).

Acts 10:34–35 says, "So Peter opened his mouth and said: 'Truly I understand that God shows no partiality, but in every nation anyone who fears him and does what is right is acceptable to him" (ESV).

- James 2:1 says, "My brothers, show no partiality as you hold the faith in our Lord Jesus Christ, the Lord of glory" (ESV).

- Psalm 67:4 says, "Let the nations be glad and sing for joy, for you judge the peoples with equity and guide the nations upon earth" (ESV).

And lest you think God would at least favor the poor (understandable because we know how much he values them), Leviticus 19:15 tells us, "You shall do no injustice in court. You shall not be partial to the poor or defer to the great, but in righteousness shall you judge your neighbor" (ESV). God's chief concern is that we live righteously, following his ways and walking in his love. Why? Because then we will be able to live in relationship with him and peaceably with everyone else.

Our shared creation in God's image, our shared need for the blood of Jesus, and our shared destiny and inheritance in him, makes us equal in God's sight and should make us equal in one another's sight.

Galatians 3:26–29 says:

> So in Christ Jesus you are all children of God through faith, for all of you who were baptized into Christ have clothed yourselves with Christ. There is neither Jew nor Gentile, neither slave nor free, nor is there male and female, for you are all one in Christ Jesus. If you belong to Christ, then you are Abraham's seed, and heirs according to the promise.
> (NIV)

What we must understand is that as God's children, we *have* equality. God sees color when it comes to his beautiful and creative work of forming so many cultures and nations. And when it comes to equity, God doesn't limit access to salvation or eternal life. God sees his precious children who he created. He knows better than anyone, even us, what he has created us to be. When we walk in relationship with him and follow his ways, he leads us to our eternal destiny. He brings about the fullness of our true potential that he placed within us from the very beginning.

Proverbs 2:1–15 paints us a beautiful picture of what equity is all about:

> My son, if you accept my words and store up my commands within you, turning your ear to wisdom and applying your heart to understanding—indeed, if you call out for insight and cry aloud for understanding, and if you look for it as for silver and search for it as for hidden treasure, then you will understand the fear of the LORD and find the knowledge of God.

> For the LORD gives wisdom; from his mouth come knowledge and understanding. He holds success in store for the upright, he is a shield to those whose walk is blameless, for he guards the course of the just and protects the way of his faithful ones. Then you will understand what is right and just and fair—every good path. For wisdom will enter your heart, and knowledge will be pleasant to your soul. Discretion will protect you, and understanding will guard you. Wisdom will save you from the ways of wicked men, from men whose words are perverse, who have left the straight paths to walk in dark ways, who delight in doing wrong and rejoice in the perverseness of evil, whose paths are crooked and who are devious in their ways. (NIV)

Favoritism is the same thing as partiality. We can understand the word "partiality" by reviewing some definitions of the term. Merriam Webster's *Dictionary* defines "partial" as "biased to one party; inclined to favor one party in a cause, or one side of a question, more than the other; not indifferent." A second meaning emphasizes favoring something "without reason," and a third, "affecting a part only; not general or universal; not total," implies dividing or separating things apart from the whole.

An excellent way to understand how the Bible uses the word is to look at different translations of James 2:1. In the *International Standard Version*, the word partiality is used. In the *New International Version*, we see the word favoritism. In the *Good News Translation*, it says, "You must never treat people in different ways according to their outward appearance." And the *Amplified Bible* reads, "My brethren, pay no servile regard to people [show no prejudice, no partiality]. Do not [attempt to] hold [and] practice the faith of our Lord Jesus Christ, [the Lord] of Glory, [together with snobbery]!"

The word used in the original Greek of the New Testament is προσωποληψία (*prosopolepsia*). This word means [3]"the fault of one who when called on to give judgment has the respect of the outward circumstances of man and not to their intrinsic merits, and so prefers, as the more worthy, one who is rich, high born, or powerful, to another who does not have these qualities."

Racial, social, religious, and political prejudices always have and will continue to exist in our world. These prejudices can be extremely dangerous when some become radical in their beliefs and violent in their actions. The good news is that although prejudices have always existed in human nature, as we are fallen and sinful, through the power we receive in Christ, we can overcome them.

Sadly, prejudices exist on the intellectual level as well. Those with degrees of varying kinds often look down upon those without them. Many will value the opinions of highly educated people more than others. Some people with these degrees allow it to build up pride within them, acting in a snobby way toward others. Sadly, we see this in every sphere of life, even in the Church.

In the Church, we also see the "holier than thou" people who flaunt their spiritually in an effort to seem more righteous than others. They will often criticize others for their lack of pi-

---

[3] 11 G4382 - prosōpolēmpsia - Strong's Greek Lexicon (mgnt). Blue Letter Bible. (n.d.). Retrieved July 5, 2022, from https://www.blueletterbible.org/lexicon/g4382/mgnt/mgnt/0-1/ `

ety instead of encouraging them in the love and grace of Jesus. This is the bias known as "self-righteousness."

But Didn't God Show Favoritism?

Many will argue that God showed favoritism toward his chosen people, the Israelites, in the Old Testament. In ancient times, it does seem as if God showed favoritism toward the Israelites, and only they could receive salvation. From our perspective today, we know that he was working solely through Israel only for that time, preparing a people for the coming of Jesus, who would bring salvation to all. But this should not be surprising. God has always used the concept of "vicariousness." Adam was the first man, and so he was a representative. This is why his sin was so devastating for the human race and the earth he'd been given charge of. "As in Adam, all die…" (1 Cor 15:22).

When God wanted to save the human race, he chose another vicarious man who he had found to be righteous, Noah. Then, the next phase of God's plan to bless all nations came through a vicarious man, Abraham, which led to the vicarious Jews, which led to the ultimate vicarious man, Jesus Christ, born of the virgin Mary. If God ever seemed to show favoritism, it was so that he could bless each and every one of his creatures, particularly his human creatures, his image bearers, his children. "For as in Adam all die, so in Christ shall all be made alive" (1 Cor 15:22 NIV).

In short, when it comes to equity, God is for anyone who will come to him. "Whoever" believes shall not perish but shall have eternal life.

Bias in Biblical Interpretation

There has been an unsettling dialogue in recent years to point out that all of us have some bias regarding how we view Scripture. Some hear this and think, "of course, how could we not?" Others hear this and get upset: "The Bible is perfect. It cannot be misunderstood or misinterpreted by the *truly saved*." Then they use that belief as a litmus test. If someone doesn't believe what they believe about every secondary or tertiary issue, they must not be a Christian because "they don't believe the Bible."

But think for yourself about this. Isn't it simply logic that tells us people are going to read any book, the Bible included, with a cultural lens? Consider the early Church in Jerusalem. They all knew the Old Testament, and many of them had known Jesus Christ personally. But when it came to the Gentiles and how to practice their new faith, they disagreed harshly. Previously, I said that Peter was enlightened by the Holy Spirit regarding the inclusion of the Gentiles into the Church. But in Antioch, the Jewish Christians who opposed the idea intimidated him to the point where he shrank back from fellowshipping with the Gentile Christians. We know this because Paul had to call him out. He basically had to tell him,

> "Stop being biased!" (Gal 2:11–13)

Think about your own experiences, views, and cultural lens. Can't you imagine how you could be reading the Bible through a personal lens? In an interview with *Christianity Today*, scholar and historian Christopher Hall explains that one way to begin to overcome cultural biases today would be to study the early church's interpretation of Scripture, who lived at a time much closer to when the biblical events happened and were recorded. If we do this, we can at least try to understand the original context for the Holy Spirit–inspired writing. When asked how to begin to study the Bible with less bias, [4]Hall says:

> Well, if we want to be effective Bible readers, we will immerse ourselves in the life of the church—we will be in church Sunday and in contact with our church community outside of Sundays as well.
>
> We will immerse ourselves, too, in the history of the church, because the Holy Spirit has a history. We will be willing to develop listening skills—to push on through the dissonance that we all experience when we first step outside our linguistic, cultural, and historical boundaries.
>
> The Fathers would also tell us that we must know the whole story from beginning to end. Maybe allowing the end of the story to penetrate earlier aspects of the story.
>
> We will be developing specific virtues that will enable us to interpret Scripture well—not just a finely tuned mind but also a finely tuned heart. For example, the Fathers set great store in maintaining an attitude of humility as one read the text.
>
> Finally, we will surround our reading with prayer. Prayer was the sine qua non of the Fathers in understanding Scripture.

---

4   Christopher A. Hall, "The Habits of Highly Effective Bible Readers," Christian History | Learn the History of Christianity & the Church (Christian History, October 1, 2003), https://www.christianitytoday.com/history/issues/issue-80/habits-of-highly-effective-bible-readers.html.

You cannot know what the Bible is saying, they tell us, unless you are conversing with its author.

To summarize in bullets:

- Start engaging with the people in your church outside of Sunday morning.
- Immerse yourself in Church history to see how people understood context in different eras, particularly the very early Church.
- Understand the redemptive story of the Bible front to back and put everything else within that context.
- Strive for humility as you engage Scripture.
- Pray!

Dealing with bias in the Church and the world starts with acknowledging it.

For the Church to continue growing healthy and strong, we must eliminate prejudice and bias from our midst. If it continues to exist and grow, the Church will not move into the future in a way pleasing to God, and we will fail in the attempt to worship and live among diverse cultures within the Church.

CHAPTER FOUR:

The Diversity in the Very Earliest Church: The Twelve

Diversity and inclusion are demonstrated in the Gospels, even by Jesus' choice of disciples. The people who made up Jesus' inner circle were not one and the same kind. They came from different backgrounds, experiences, and social statuses. This is powerful because it means the seedling of the Church of Jesus Christ was as diverse as can be, and it removes any excuse we may have for why our churches must be homogeneous.

In this chapter, I'll prove it. We are going to explore each of the disciples and what they can teach us about DEI.

Peter
Peter, known as Simon, son of Jonas before Jesus changed his name to Peter, was a fisherman. He was from Bethsaida and

Capernaum. His legacy was bringing the message of the Gospel as far as Babylon. He evangelized and did missionary work for the remainder of his life after following Jesus. However, he never turned back to his previous life as a fisherman.

Peter also wrote two books of the New Testament: First and Second Peter. Tradition tells us Peter was crucified in Rome. Refusing to be executed the same way as Jesus, he insisted on being crucified upside down. Every list giving us the names of the disciples lists Peter first. That's how highly regarded he is among the disciples.

Peter had his faults, as we all do. He denied Jesus three times when Jesus needed him most. We see many stories throughout the Scriptures where Peter failed time and time again. But Peter had a good heart and loved the Lord, seeking His forgiveness and coming back stronger after each failure.

Peter is a prime example of someone who settles his sin and moves on to freedom in the Lord. When we meet him early on, he is a fisherman who comes to follow Jesus. But even during his time with Jesus, he is constantly doubting, messing up, and not living out his true potential. He shows his human nature frequently and in every way. One profound example of this is the story of Jesus walking on water. The disciples find themselves on their boat amidst a terrifying storm. We must deeply consider their dire situation to let this story sink in. They weren't on the water in a luxury boat of our times. They weren't even in a modest boat of our times. It had little to no defense against such brutal weather. Imagine the kind of boat a poor fisherman would own in those times. How would it hold up in the face of a fierce and battering storm?

In this light, it's completely understandable why they would be terrified while trying to survive such a storm. The winds and waves battered their humble boat, and they must have felt as if it was just a matter of time until they would meet their watery demise. But Jesus was not only coming to save them, Jesus was coming to show them what legendary feats they were also capable of doing.

No doubt you've heard repeatedly about how Jesus walked on water. But do you ever hear people talk about how Peter walked on water? Matthew 14:28–29 reads, "'Lord, if it's you,' Peter replied, 'tell me to come to you on the water.' 'Come,' he said. Then Peter got down out of the boat, walked on the water and came toward Jesus.*"* It's amazing that Jesus walked on water, yes, but we've come to see Him do many miraculous things. The essential part of this story is that through the power of Jesus, Peter was able to do the miraculous as well.

Even though Peter could do something so amazing through Jesus, he needed time for it to sink in and to grasp the full potential within himself. This powerful moment for Peter happens after he spends time with the resurrected Christ and Jesus forgives him for denying Him in His time of trial. He then commissions Peter to continue His work on earth and establish His church.

There's something else beautiful that happens here. John 21:15-17 reads:

> When they had finished eating, Jesus said to Simon Peter, "Simon son of John, do you love me more than these?" "Yes, Lord," he said, "you know that I love you." Jesus said, "Feed my lambs." Again Jesus said, "Simon son of John, do you love me?" He answered, "Yes, Lord, you know that I love you." Jesus said, "Take care of my sheep." The third time he said to him, "Simon son of John, do you love me?" Peter was hurt because Jesus asked him the third time, "Do you love me?" He said, "Lord, you know all things; you know that I love you." Jesus said, "Feed my sheep."

Through this encounter, Peter settles his sin. Then, drawing upon the power of Jesus and the mission passed onto him, he goes out into the world and does remarkable things. Next, we see him preaching so powerfully at Pentecost that the Bible says three thousand people became followers of Jesus that day. Acts 2:41 reads, "Those who accepted his message were baptized, and about three thousand were added to their number that day." Think about the joy and accomplishment we feel in our ministry when one person comes to faith.

Peter showed us the incredible power of diversity in his ministry of spreading the Gospel. When Peter preached at Pentecost, his message was so powerful that the Holy Spirit came down among the people. People from all over came to hear Peter's preaching, people of many nations and languages. But when the Holy Spirit came down among them, they all heard the message in their own language.

This beautiful story shows us unity in the midst of diversity. Despite their differences, the power of their unity through the Holy Spirit brought about one of the most miraculous moments recorded in biblical history. Three thousand people came to the saving knowledge of Jesus Christ that day, and those three thousand people were all from different places and spoke other languages.

This example gives us a blueprint for working with diverse populations. God desires that we would come together to learn about him, worship him, and bring others to faith by following the leading of the Holy Spirit. God desires that all his children come together, despite their differences, to bring about the powerful manifestations we saw at Pentecost.

James

James was the brother of John the Apostle. A fisherman by trade, he hailed from Bethsaida, Capernaum, and Jerusalem. Sadly, Herod beheaded James in AD 44 (Acts 12:1,2). However, he and his brother were so close that the Bible never mentions James apart from John. Of the twelve disciples, he was the first to become a martyr.

James and John were known as "the sons of thunder" because of their explosive tempers. We can imagine they must have struggled to hold back those tempers when faced with diversity. For instance, when Jesus and His disciples enter Samaria, who were bitter enemies of the Jews, James' temper must have been flaring. Sometimes we must fight against the dispositions and biases taught to us growing up and embrace God's vision for diversity. James was able to do that and stands as a powerful example.

John

John is known as the beloved disciple. Born to Zebedee and Salome, he was brother to the disciple James. He was a fisherman like his brother. He wrote the Gospel of John, I John, II John, III John, and Revelation. He ministered to the churches in Asia Minor. He was also the only apostle banished to the Isle of Patmos. He was also the only apostle that was not martyred.

John and James' family were a bit wealthier than those of the other Apostles. We see this in Mark 1:20, which tells us that he hired servants to aid in his fishing business. In light of this, the brothers may have felt a sense of entitlement above the other Apostles. Coupled with their temperament, I'm sure this often led to conflict among them.

We see this a lot in our society today. Our socioeconomic status can affect how we view ourselves and others. We must be careful to avoid this pitfall. This kind of bias creates division among us, grows pride within our hearts, and separates us from the path God has called us to walk down. James and John overcame this bias and sense of entitlement: We should follow their powerful example.

Andrew

Andrew was Peter's brother. He, too, was a fisherman before following Jesus. Matthew 4:18–20 says, "As Jesus was walking beside the Sea of Galilee, he saw two brothers, Simon called Peter and his brother Andrew. They were casting a net into the lake, for they were fishermen. 'Come, follow me,' Jesus said, 'and I will send you out to fish for people.'" At once they left their nets and followed him.

This passage gives us the model for obedience to the call of God above any other priorities in life. Becoming a "fisher of men" was more important than his earthly occupation.

Andrew had a passion for bringing others to the life-saving knowledge of Christ. Jesus had changed his life, and he desired others to experience that profound change as well. Tradition tells us that Andrew died a martyr of the faith, following through on his convictions until the end.

Bartholomew or Nathanael
Bartholomew, also known as Nathanael, son of Talmai, was from Cana of Galilee. As a missionary, Bartholomew would have interacted with all kinds of people from around the world. And as a disciple, he would have seen firsthand how Jesus treated everyone with love and respect. Likewise, as we go about our ministries, we will encounter all kinds of people. We must act toward them the same way that Jesus would: as a reflection of God's immeasurable and never-ending love.

It's also worth noting that we only know a little about Bartholomew, as his name is mentioned only in the four lists of the disciples (Matthew 10:2–4, Mark 3:16–19, Luke 6:14–16, Acts 1:1–13).

We can learn a lesson in humble obedience from Bartholomew. He was engaged in the same work as the other disciples without being recognized or called out for his specific contributions. How many of us are willing to fulfill our call to ministry to unreached people in quiet, reverent obedience?

James, the Lesser

The disciple James is also known as James the Lesser. He was born to Alpheus and Mary in Galilee. The Apostle Jude was his brother. He is the author of the book of James in the New Testament. He is known to have preached in Palestine and Egypt; his life ended in martyrdom like many other disciples.

Some scholars have found reason to believe him to be the brother of the Apostle Matthew, though they lack hard evidence as we know very little about James. If this is true, it brings up some interesting thoughts of acceptance. Matthew was a tax collector for the Romans, making him hated and treasonous in the eyes of his people. His family likely shunned him, including James. Yet Jesus' love would have brought them back to unity under Him, showing James, and us today, that everyone is worthy of God's love.

Judas

Judas Iscariot is well-known for all the wrong reasons. Born in Kerioth of Judah to a man named Simon, his background may have caused some uncomfortableness among Jesus' other disciples as they all hailed from Galilee. Nevertheless, his story shows us that we are all one in Jesus, no matter our origins. Therefore, we should never keep our distance from anyone based on where they are born.

Although Judas became a disciple of Jesus, ultimately, he betrayed Him in a shocking and saddening fashion. Before he followed Christ, he was a zealous Jewish nationalist, fighting for Jewish independence from Rome.

Judas was the keeper of the disciples' funds. Sadly, the Bible tells us that he often took their money for his own selfish benefit. It seems he struggled to follow Jesus wholeheartedly the whole time he was with Him. Still, Jesus loved him and served him, even washing his feet at the Last Supper. Jesus did this, even for someone he knew would betray Him. Jesus looked past Judas' sin and loved the person God created underneath it all.

Jude or Thaddeus
Jude was also known as Thaddeus or Lebbeus. His parents were Alpheus and Mary, shared by his brother James. Little is known of Jude compared to the knowledge we have of most of the other disciples. We know that before becoming a disciple of Jesus, Jude was a Jewish nationalist. These nationalists were known for taking violent action against the Romans who ruled over them.

While they were passionate about their cause, they misunderstood God's directive on attaining their freedom. Instead of resorting to violence, they needed to embrace the life-saving knowledge and presence of Jesus. Thankfully, Jude learns this and lives it out beautifully in his life. Jude gives an example to us all to love everyone and trust God to intervene when evil people oppress others. Never forget that Jesus prayed even for those who had persecuted Him and nailed Him to the cross.

Matthew or Levi
Matthew, also known as Levi, lived in Capernaum. He was a tax collector who became a follower of Jesus and wrote the Gospel of Matthew. He died a martyr in Ethiopia. Matthew's name means "a gift of God," showing his intrinsic value in God's eyes despite how the people viewed him as a tax collector.

The Jewish people saw the tax collectors as unjust sinners. It was a rough world to live in and extremely difficult to make a living. So when the Romans came around seeking to take what little money they had, it was infuriating to the people, understandably so. Consider Matthew for a moment. He was a tax collector for the Romans and a Jewish man himself. That was treason in the eyes of his people, and they saw him as a servant of Rome instead of one of their own.

You can imagine the conflict that must have ensued when Jesus called Matthew to join the disciples. How must they have felt? Someone they saw as an ungodly criminal was now part of their group and was supposed to be their equal. They would learn that they were all the same under Christ, and Matthew became the first to write a Gospel telling their story.

Philip

Philip was born and lived in Bethsaida, the same town as Peter and Andrew. Philip gives us a great example of how we treat others who think differently than we do. Instead of arguing with Nathaniel over their conflicting beliefs, he simply lets Nathaniel see for himself. We should follow his example, never forcing our thoughts or beliefs upon others but rather letting them see and decide for themselves.

Simon the Zealot

Simon, the Zealot, lived in Galilee. Unfortunately, all we know about him is that he was a Zealot. The Zealots were Jewish nationalists who fought against Rome. The Zealots saw Rome's rule over them as an oppression of God's people and believed they needed to take up arms to fight back against the Romans.

Simon was devoted to God's Law but sadly misinterpreted it, as violence is never the answer. Thankfully, he found the peace of Christ and a new way to impact the lives of God's people for the better. His hatred for Rome turned into a love for all people, as taught to him by Jesus. Instead of being a man who fought against others, he became a man who served others. We can learn a lot from his example.

Thomas
Thomas, the disciple, came from Galilee. Tradition says he worked for the cause of the Gospel across the known world. However, everything we know about Thomas comes exclusively from the Gospel of John, where in John 20:25, he refuses to believe in Jesus until he sees the wounds in Jesus' side and hands. This story is where he receives the nickname he is known by: "Doubting Thomas." Thomas went from a doubting man to a man of devout faith. It's natural for us all to doubt or question things at one point or another. What matters is, like Thomas, we accept Jesus' reassurance and continue to walk with Him.

Jesus' disciples give us an interesting analogy. All twelve of them were common Jewish men living out regular lives. The heaviness and responsibility of life weighed them down even as they walked with Christ. As a result, they still needed to settle their souls and boldly walk into the fullness of their potential. Many of us may find ourselves in a similar place today.

I have aimed to show that the disciples were diverse in many ways. Consider the vastly different backgrounds. There are also stark differences in how sin manifested in their lives before and after Jesus called them to follow him. If we are going to have churches that reflect this sort of diversity, there is only one answer, Jesus. He is the one unifying force. He is the common denominator in any diverse group of Christians. And Christ connects white churches, Black churches, underground house churches, rich churches, and poor churches. Wherever the name of Jesus is preached, the potential for a healthy, diverse body of believers is possible.

CHAPTER FIVE:

God's Heart for Love

How Do We Follow God's Plan for Inclusion?

Start with love.

> Jesus said to love our neighbor as we love ourselves (Mark 12:31).

So then, we must examine our love for ourselves to have a foundation for love of others.

It's easy to say "God loves me," but do we truly mean it? Understanding the depths of God's love is critical in our development of understanding who we are and what we're called to do. Our identity and purpose are crucial to our lives and must be firmly rooted in our understanding of God's love.

We all can agree that we know God loves everyone. He has to, after all: He's God! But sometimes, taking that truth and making it personal is hard. While it's easy to say and understand that God loves everyone, it can be much harder to embrace the fact that God has that same abundant love for us personally. Nonetheless, God loves us each day for the unique and beautiful individuals he created us to be.

How does this flesh itself out in our lives? First, it affects our interactions with God, others, and even ourselves. We gain so much when we truly accept God's unconditional love for us. We become more confident in our calling; we become more loving and compassionate toward others; we experience abundant peace in our hearts and so much more.

That all happens because God's love is so profound in our lives that it completely transforms us from the inside out. As God's love surges through us, we begin the journey of sanctification that leads us to become more and more like Christ. The Holy Spirit leads us on an adventure that guides us straight to the destined purpose and identity God prepared for us before we were even born.

There is no greater expression of God's love than what Jesus accomplished on the cross for us. 1 John 3:16 says,

> "By this we know love, that he laid down his life for us, and we ought to lay down our lives for the brothers" (ESV).

Jesus took on the full impact of death in our place to cover our sins once and for all. He did this so that we could have the profound relationship with God that we experience today. God was willing to make that incredible sacrifice because he'd do anything to be an intimate part of your life. That's how much he loves you.

John 3:16 says, "For God so loved the world that he gave his one and only Son, that whoever believes in him shall not perish but have eternal life" (NIV). Let the story of Jesus' redemptive work on the cross permeate your heart. Meditate on it daily. Realize the immense cost that God paid to make a relationship with you possible. Honor Jesus' sacrifice by investing deeply in your relationship with God. Let his love come to define your life in every way.

When we speak of loving yourself from a biblical perspective, *I am not implying loving yourself at the expense of others.* Nor do I suggest the arrogant narcissism that plagues our world. Instead, I'm talking about a healthy understanding of our identity in Christ Jesus.

Jesus said, "You must love the Lord your God with all your heart, all your soul, and all your mind." This is the first and greatest commandment. A second is equally important:

> "Love your neighbor as yourself."

The entire law and all the demands of the prophets are based on these two commandments. (Mt 22:37–40 NLT)

God's love for you is so great that you should see a reflection of that love when you look in the mirror. God loves you when you're at the top of your game or in your lowest moments, no matter your regrets and shame. His love is not limited to what you can or cannot do or what you did or did not do.

Honestly, ask yourself this question: If God loves me as much as he does, what excuse do I have *not* to love myself? God has made you in his image. That in and of itself is more than enough reason to love yourself. Loving yourself has nothing to do with what you do or don't do; it's all about honoring what God created in you. He made you from an overflow of his love and finds you irreplaceable.

Embrace the love God has for you and extend love to yourself as well. When you love yourself as Jesus commands, you can genuinely love others. The love God gives us will then flow through us and into the lives of others. This chain of events will win more and more hearts for Jesus and allow the world to experience the profound love and unity that a relationship with God offers.

Love what God loves. God loves you!

Paul's simple thesis in 1st Corinthians 14 is profound: "Let love be your highest goal." I think of how often love is not the highest goal in our lives. We quickly get consumed with other things and believe we are walking in love because we're not exploding in anger at someone. But there's much more to love than just holding back rage. We must strive for something higher than that.

Love is a verb and demands action. For the only inspiration we'll ever need, let's look to Jesus' perfect example. How did Jesus express God's love to others? He served them and sought to meet their needs in every way. Matthew 20:28 says,

> "For even the Son of Man came not to be served but to serve others and to give his life as a ransom for many" (NLT).

Let this verse soak in for a moment. Jesus completely flipped the world's logic on its head. When someone with power and authority shows us attention, nine out of ten times they demand our service. But Jesus was different. Instead of using his power and authority to accept preferential treatment, Jesus chose to use that same power and authority to change the lives of everyone. Jesus is our prime example of what it means to act meaningfully in response to God's outpouring of love in our lives.

Here is where things get tricky and why it is so hard to talk about loving ourselves rightly. Even though most people suffer from some degree of self-loathing, one of the biggest pitfalls we succumb to is our society's idolatrous focus on the self. We are brought up from a young age to do everything we can to be successful, wealthy, and to get ahead at all costs. But that's not the way of the Gospel. That's not how Jesus lived his life! Jesus lived his life for others, and that's how he calls us to live our lives as well. In doing so, we powerfully reflect his love.

As you read the Gospels, you see that Jesus is constantly serving others, often at the expense of himself. He spends his time preaching the Good News, teaching his disciples, and healing those in desperate need. Jesus does the miraculous time and time again, investing deeply of his time and energy to make sure that others are taken care of. Jesus was not seeking fame, fortune, or security; his eyes were solely focused on building up the Kingdom of God.

Jesus was so focused on showing God's love to the world that he was willing to give all of himself, even his very life, to illustrate what showing love to others truly means. Jesus' redemptive work on the cross shows that love must be put into action to change the world.

We are called to emulate His example. In Matthew 16:24, Jesus says,

> "If any of you wants to be my follower, you must give up your way, take up your cross, and follow me" (NLT).

Jesus is telling us through this verse that we must be willing to act in the lives of others in a loving way, no matter the cost. Our sole focus must be on showing everyone we encounter the life-altering love of God.

Paul said,

> For Christ's love compels us, because we are convinced that one died for all, and therefore all died. And he died for all, that those who live should no longer live for themselves but for him who died for them and was raised again. (2 Cor 5:14–15 NIV)

A little later he adds, "We are therefore Christ's ambassadors, as though God were making his appeal through us. We implore you on Christ's behalf: Be reconciled to God" (2 Cor 5:20 NIV). This means that God's love compels us to show his love to others. How will Jesus demonstrate to the hurting world that he loves them? Through you and me.

What is your highest goal? Is it that next raise or promotion? The fulfillment of a particular dream? A certain sense of security?

Let *love* be your highest goal, even if it means great sacrifice. That's the way of the Gospel and what our faith is truly all about. Doing so will teach you what it means to live in and genuinely reflect God's love. You will find that living in God's love is more glorious than anything you had to sacrifice to make it happen in the first place.

Be honest in your evaluation of your priorities. Ask God to help you refocus your worldview so that your highest goal will be to display the love of God to the world. Jesus said that others would know we belong to him by the way we love (John 13:35). There is no better place to do that than among people who are vastly different from us. There is no one that you and I are not called to love. If Jesus said we are to love our enemies, then we are most certainly to love our brothers and sisters in the Church from other cultures and backgrounds.

But it's hard to walk in love when we don't understand what love is. It is a shame how cavalier we are today with the word love. We say we love a particular sports team, we love tacos, we love movies. Yet, in the same breath, we love our families and our God. We overuse and undervalue the true depth of the word's meaning.

Let me ask: How did your spouse and kids get put on the same level with movies and tacos?

It seems that, culturally, love is regulated to mere emotions that can be fleeting. I've witnessed couples walk away from relationships because they "fell out of love." Sadly, it happens all the time! What their words really mean is that the emotional passion has dwindled. It's a shame. Ask any older couple who has been married for a long time, and they will attest to this thought. Sometimes the passion goes down, but if you stick with it, on the other side is a passion that is beyond description. Many never discover the joys of this because they equate passion and love as the same.

That's not to say that there aren't emotions involved in love. There absolutely are. But emotions are not the total of what it means to love.

You see, love is not a first feeling. It's not uncontrollable. It's not what the world makes it out to be. Godly love is so remarkably different from what we find portrayed in the world. Godly love is counter-cultural. God's example of love is unconditional and never fading. God never "falls out of love" with anyone, not even when we disobey and go against him again and again. Love is proactive. Godly love says, "I'm not going to wait for a feeling before I react." Romans 5:8 says, "But God showed his great love for us by sending Christ to die for us while we were still sinners" (NLT).

God didn't wait for us to return to him before saving us. He saved us even though our hearts were far from him. Why's that? Because he loves us anyway, despite anything we've ever done.

In 1 Corinthians 13:4–7, Paul describes what true, godly love is all about: "Love is patient and kind. Love is not jealous or boastful or proud or rude. It does not demand its own way. It is not irritable, and it keeps no record of being wronged. It does not rejoice about injustice but rejoices whenever the truth wins out. Love never gives up, never loses faith, is always hopeful, and endures through every circumstance" (NLT).

Love is: patient, kind, forgiving, honest, secure, trust, hopes, and persistent. Love is not: jealous, arrogant, rude, selfish, or irritable. Love is not based upon the condition of your emotion. Love persists through all circumstances. That's because love is more powerful than anything you will ever face. Godly love conquers all because it is stronger than any fleeting emotion that arises in your heart.

Love is the opposite of what we make it out to be. Don't run to movies, television, or romantic novels when looking for real examples of love. That emotionally fueled, chaotic love is not what real love is all about. If you want to see the true definition of what it means to love and be loved, dive deeply into your Bible and read the miraculous story of God's everlasting love.

Biblical love is the foundation for genuine Christ-centered relationships. In biblical love, there is room for true diversity.

1 Corinthians 13:1–7:

> If I speak in the tongues of men and of angels, but have not love, I am only a ringing gong or a clanging cymbal. If I have the gift of prophecy and can fathom all mysteries and all knowledge, and if I have absolute faith so as to move mountains, but have not love, I am nothing. If I give all I possess to the poor and exult in the surrender of my body, but have not love, I gain nothing.

> Love is patient, love is kind. It does not envy, it does not boast, it is not proud. It is not rude, it is not self-seeking, it is not easily angered, it keeps no account of wrongs. Love takes no pleasure in evil but rejoices in the truth. It bears all things, believes all things, hopes all things, endures all things. (BSB)

PART Two

COMMIT TO A WAY FORWARD

In part two of this book, I will outline the COMMIT framework for bringing about diversity, equity, and inclusion.

COMMIT stands for:

Chapter Six: Commit to Courageous Action (for Family, Church, the World)

Chapter Seven: Open Your Eyes and Ears (to the Good, the Bad, and the Ugly)

Chapter Eight: Move Beyond Lip Service

Chapter Nine: Make Room for Controversy and Conflict

Chapter Ten: Invite New Perspectives

Chapter Eleven: Tell the Truth Even When It Hurts

CHAPTER SIX:

Commit to Courageous Action (for Family, Church, the World)

The C in the COMMIT framework stands for Commit to Courageous Action. In short, nothing groundbreaking or difficult happens by accident and without intention.

In order to commit to courageous action that is based on sound biblical principles, we must carefully discern what are God's commands versus man's religious traditions. What we cannot do is predict all outcomes and control for outcomes. All we can do, and all God asks of us, is to commit to a certain courageous and compassionate way of being. For an example of what this can look like consider Jesus in Matthew 12:3–8.

Jesus' disciples were walking through the grain fields on the Sabbath day, and they were picking the heads of grain to rub together into a snack because they were hungry. Some of the Pharisees witnessed this and were upset because they seemed to be "working on the Sabbath," which to their way of interpreting the law, was unlawful. To their religious consciousness, it would be far better to starve than to do this "work" on the day of rest.

> Jesus responded, "Haven't you ever read what King David and his men did when they were hungry? They entered the house of God and ate the sacred bread of God's presence, violating the law by eating bread that only the priests were allowed to eat. And haven't you read in the Torah that the priests violated the rules of the Sabbath by carrying out their duties in the temple on a Saturday, and yet they are without blame? But I say to you, there is one here who is even greater than the temple. If only you could learn the meaning of the words 'I want compassion more than a sacrifice,' you wouldn't be condemning my innocent disciples. For the Son of Man exercises his lordship over the Sabbath." (The Passion Translation TPT)

It is so much easier to stick to the letter of the law rather than discerning the spirit of the law. If we discern the spirit of the laws of God, particularly to love him with all our heart, soul, and strength, and to love our neighbor as ourselves, then it opens up a host of opportunities for commitment to courageous action.

Sadly, some godly action requires courage because it will draw heat from the religious. This is what we can expect when we COMMIT to diversity, equity, and inclusion in our churches, our lives, and our hearts.

Trust God for the Outcomes

One obstacle for many people is the fact that they cannot see the outcome. They cannot predict the future, so they work and work to try to sort out what might happen if they do this and what might happen if they do that, and they fail to act at all. Trying to control outcomes is idolatry because it is God's job to control outcomes.

Satan wanted Christ to control outcomes when he tempted him in the wilderness. A summary of their conversation could be as follows: "Jesus, you know you are the King of the world, you know you are going to have all this anyway. Why not make it happen now? Why not compromise your principles a little? After all, isn't it the outcome that matters?"

Satan would have us not trust God. So often we can't see exactly what God is doing and how he is doing it. But the beautiful truth is, we don't have to. God always has a plan, but the only way for us to be useful to him in that plan is to make ourselves available *regardless of the outcome*. What do we need to know? We simply need to know what is right. We need to know what is biblical. We need to know what God wants, and he has no problem telling us.

Imagine Jesus' disciples watching him work. We can see from the Gospels that they rarely understood what he was doing or agreed with it. Like everyone else, they did not want a dying Savior. They wanted instead a conquering king. They wanted him to put some of his miraculous powers to work earning respect for himself and his associates. That's what they wanted. That was not what God wanted.

Instead, Jesus was committed to principles, especially the guiding principle of "I do what I see the Father doing," (Jn 5:19) and "not my will but yours be done" (Lk 22:42). No one could have predicted the outcome, but God knew the ultimate outcome was nothing less than the restoration of the world and the ultimate defeat of Satan, sin, darkness, and death.

Commit to Courage

How then do we apply this to the goal of this book to partner with God for a greater and more God-exalting DEI in our churches? What are our guiding principles?

First, they must mirror those of Christ. We must be committed to obeying God. DEI is biblical. Love between people groups is biblical. Demolition of the "dividing wall of hostility" between peoples is biblical. Courageously standing up to racism, classism, and other isms is biblical. This is a lifelong journey, and we trust God and the Holy Spirit to lead us all into truth.

We don't have to know everything to have a positive impact. We have to obey God's calling, trusting the Holy Spirit's leading, and relying on God's provision to see us through.

I will reiterate here the fact that I don't have all the answers to some of the complex issues surrounding the intersection of the body of Christ and DEI. No one except for God does. But this book is the beginning of a long overdue conversation. For now, let's focus on doing what we all know to do based on explicit instruction in the Word of God—love each other.

Sometimes it can be intimidating to take a stand for Christ, especially in situations where people have differing and strong opinions. But that's God's specialty. As we said, Jesus was not popular or widely accepted in his ministry as he challenged religious traditions.

Before you despair trying to come up with global initiatives and world fame as a change maker, consider these simple actions that require courageous commitment:

- Someone tells an offensive joke about "foreigners" at the dinner table, not knowing the new neighbors you invited are immigrants. Do you say anything? What do you say?
- Your church is invited to join a city-wide faith coalition, and one of the leaders says, "We don't go to that side of town." What do you do?
- The world is enraged with yet another act of terror. People in your congregation and in the broader community are looking to your church for refuge and direction. How do you engage? Do you engage?

Principle: Lead with Compassion

Just because we are committing to courageous action, doesn't mean that courage is the number one priority. The number one priority is compassion. When you yield to love and compassion, you relieve yourself of the burden of philosophical conundrums that plague so many who want to help. Different perspectives on this issue cause disharmony and a lack of unity in the body of Christ. Some want to help, others want to blame.

My perspective is, "It doesn't matter why someone is hungry. Let's just get them something to eat, and we can sort out the rest later." Even Jesus wouldn't minister to the people while they were hungry. He fed them first. John 6:5–11 tells us,

> When Jesus looked up and saw a great crowd coming toward him, he said to Philip, "Where shall we buy bread for these people to eat?" He asked this only to test him, for he already had in mind what he was going to do.
>
> Philip answered him, "It would take more than half a year's wages to buy enough bread for each one to have a bite!"
>
> Another of his disciples, Andrew, Simon Peter's brother, spoke up, "Here is a boy with five small barley loaves and two small fish, but how far will they go among so many?"
>
> Jesus said, "Have the people sit down." There was plenty of grass in that place, and they sat down (about five thousand men were there). Jesus then took the loaves, gave thanks, and distributed to those who were seated as much as they wanted. He did the same with the fish. (NIV)

Or consider what John said,

> This is how we know what love is: Jesus Christ laid down his life for us. And we ought to lay down our lives for our brothers and sisters.

> If anyone has material possessions and sees a brother or sister in need but has no pity on them, how can the love of God be in that person? (1 Jn 3:16–17 NIV)

When Jesus faced the five thousand, he didn't ask the people who were hungry and without any food, "Why have you come here without provisions?" Or "What have you done to try to get your own food?" Or "Why should this child have to share his food with all of these able-bodied adults?"

Discerning the "Bootstrap" Mindset and Victimhood

As believers we can consciously choose to lean in with compassion. Remember when Jesus healed the crippled man? He healed him and told him to take up his mat and walk. Many people grab onto the "take up your bed and walk" portion of John 5:1. The "pull yourself up by your own bootstraps" sentiment is rooted in a long debated "victimhood" dialogue.

A lot of people would be so focused on investigating what this man has been doing for the past thirty-eight years that they would have never healed him.

Are people investigating and philosophizing about how someone becomes destitute or whether they deserve help? This is our brother or sister who needs help at a point and time in their life. Are people caught in a cycle of poverty or addiction succumbing to a victimhood mentality? The question often asked is, "What if they just tried harder?"

Is that what God asks of us, or could there be something else going on in these situations? Could there be an opportunity to open our eyes and ears to see and hear things that may not be a part of our lived experience?

1 Corinthians 3:6-8 says,

> I planted the seed, Apollos watered it, but God has been making it grow. So neither the one who plants nor the one who waters is anything, but only God, who makes things grow. The one who plants and the one who waters have one purpose, and they will each be rewarded according to their own labor. (NIV)

The next chapter offers more perspective on this quandary. Yes, we need to think about *how* we help those in need. Yes, there is such a thing as toxic charity that hurts people more than it helps them. But too often we use this as an excuse to do nothing. This is not right, and it could end us up with the goats in Matthew 25.

The first step, then, is to *Commit*. Nothing changes unless we do something. Let's take the first step. Let's be committed to action. Even small actions make a big difference over time. So let's make it happen. Let's commit.

CHAPTER SEVEN:

Open Your Eyes and Ears (to the Good, the Bad, and the Ugly)

The next crucial step is to open your eyes and ears. See and hear what is true. Accept what is true.

John 1:1–9 says,

> In the beginning was the Word, and the Word was with God, and the Word was God. He was with God in the beginning. Through him all things were made; without him nothing was made that has been made. In him was life, and that life was **the light of all mankind**. **The light shines in the darkness**, and the darkness has not overcome it.

There was a man sent from God whose name was John. He came as **a witness to testify concerning that light,** so that through him all might believe. He himself was not the light; he came only as a **witness to the light.**

The **true light that gives light to everyone** was coming into the world. (NIV emphasis added)

Jesus Christ is called the Light. That is because he is the Truth. He sees and says what is true. John the Baptist would accept this. He would say later, "Look, the Lamb of God who takes away the sin of the world!" (Jn 1:29 NIV). John did what we are called to do—to look at the Light, and to point others to the Light. The Light is the truth. Everything about God is about shedding light on the truth. Everything about following God is about accepting the truth: the truth about the darkness in the world, the Light that is the remedy for that darkness, and the truth about ourselves and our need for God's forgiveness for our sins.

Opening our eyes to the good, bad, and the ugly is called "faithfulness to the truth." Don't look away from what is uncomfortable to know. So much evil in the world is perpetrated or allowed by those who do not desire to know what is true. Knowing the ugly means you might have to do something about it. Most people don't like the discomfort of the change that needs to happen. Societies, families, and individuals fall apart from such willful ignorance.

One author describes the experience that Bonhoeffer had in America and his observance of the racism of Christians toward Blacks.[5]

---

[5] Daniel Dei and Dennis E. Akawobsa, "Dietrich Bonhoeffer's Perspective on Racism," *HTS Teologiese Studies/Theological Studies* 78, 1(2022). (https://doi.org/10.4102/hts.v78i1.7450)

Racial tensions disrupt social life in unimaginable ways. Accordingly, most Christian denominations renounce racism in their official statements. Generally, these official statements condemn racism for being sinful, heretical, idolatrous, and contrary to God's design and plan for humanity. However, the near silence of the Christian community on recent racial tensions in westernized societies raise doubts on effective ways Christians can deal with racism. Verbal condemnation of racism in the strictest sense is good, but a corresponding action that deals with racism is better.

Dietrich Bonhoeffer's attitude towards the abusive treatment of black people in the United States of America and Jews in Germany combines verbal condemnation with effective social action to deal with racism. For Bonhoeffer, faith and action cannot be divorced from each other. He claimed that the Christian faith engages Christians in a relationship with God and other humans. The trio's interrelatedness provides a shared status that defines humanity – a communal social character. This communal social character paves the way for individuals to actualize themselves. It sets forth respect for the dignity of other individuals as the sole means to self-consciousness.

Conversely, detaching oneself from the community leads to personal failures. Racism is evil because it isolates the individual from other individuals in the community. It makes the isolated individual feel they are more important than others. Racism distorts God's design, by which all human beings are considered a united family. Bonhoeffer calls on all Christians to transform freedom and faith into civil courage to deal with racism. Every Christian has a moral duty to deal with the isolation that racism imposes on society.

Dietrich Bonhoeffer had his eyes open to the good, the bad, and the ugly. He refused to stay isolated from the issues he saw and instead engaged.

Reserve Judgment

One thing we need to do when we are going to engage in this work is reserve judgment. It is easy to judge. The harder and deeper work is to proactively give up our right to judge a person and their actions. Instead, our first priority should be to seek to understand. Being intentional about trying to understand someone's perspective does not mean we have to agree with them. It just means we are putting godly wisdom ahead of our own opinions.

The Bible says, "Judge not, that you be not judged" (Mt. 7:1 ESV). It is important that we don't rush to snap judgments. It's important that we don't just adopt everyone's opinion who is in our group. It's important to think for yourself. And most of all, it's important that we don't hate or look down on people.

What follow are examples of the good, bad, and ugly that we want to open our eyes and ears to in our faith journey.

The Good

Oh, if only the majority of the world was committed to seeing the good in the world. Sadly, so much of our media and social media algorithms are driven by outrage and negativity. But we need daily doses of the remarkable, the beautiful, the sublime, the truth. Paul says, "Whatever is good…think on these things" (Phil 4:8). This speaks of intentionality in our thinking. Being a good steward is stewarding our thoughts and keeping our minds on godly perspectives as much as possible. So, what are some of the good things we need to open our eyes to?

First is the death and resurrection of Jesus Christ to reconcile us to God and one another. We have the good news of the Gospel to share in a world that faces a tsunami of bad news daily. And God has already given us the victory through his Son, Jesus Christ. Therefore, many of the answers we need for navigating this world with so many different people, backgrounds, and cultures can be found by searching and living the Scripture with our faith community.

We have the Bible. We have pages and pages of the Word of God, inspired by the Holy Spirit, so that we can know God and his will for our lives. We have the guidance of the Holy Spirit living in us and speaking to us. We are not alone. Jesus said he would send the Helper. He said he would be with us to the very end of the age (Mt 28:20). The miracle is that we can choose to be open to see and hear what the Holy Spirit is saying about God's will for times such as this.

Life is hard, scary, and confusing, and the Bible foretells what is happening now. Some days it's hard to differentiate from the headlines at the top of the news cycle and biblical prophecy for the last days. We gain so much when we open our hearts to learn from the Holy Spirit and from others who are different from us. If we listen, there are good things to hear. If we just open our eyes, there are good things to see.

The Bad

Unfortunately, death and calamity run rampant in our society. Why is our first response to debate if we feel a person or group deserved to suffer in a tragic event instead of the natural, human response of empathy for a life that's been lost or left devastated? Why are we so quick to find a loophole for having compassion for others?

Everyone wants to be on the receiving end of mercy when we make mistakes. We all have an opportunity to increase our capacity on the giving end of mercy in challenging situations, and if we do so, we will grow spiritually.

I spent years working in an indigent clinic providing direct patient care to the houseless and uninsured in Greensboro, North Carolina during the height of the AIDS epidemic. There was so much misinformation circulating around about the ways to contract, manage, and treat the disease.

My proximity to the epidemic and its impacts was about as close as you could get as a medical professional. For example, I was pretty good at what we called "hard sticks"—people with small veins that were hard to find. I was often called away from the doctor I was working with to assist in the lab after the phlebotomist had tried to collect blood several times unsuccessfully. I remember the sheer terror I and others felt from the occasional accidental finger prick when disposing of a used needle in such a dense population of patients living with AIDS.

I also witnessed first-hand people being treated as modern day lepers. It was hard to make sense of the harsh treatment of an entire population of people living with a devastating disease and the pain I felt sitting at a hospice facility in a dimly lit room across from someone so young with AIDS suffering in the last hours of their life. That night, watching and praying for one man as he transitioned into the afterlife, is one of the many experiences that fuels my passion for change. He was more than a patient taking his last breath—he was a soul entering eternity.

The impetus for my desire to see the body of Christ open its eyes and ears to the many ways we're called to serve in an imperfect world comes from a very deep visceral place of life-altering experiences. I've seen the ugly up close and personal, and I'm confident that the love of God will help us all. How many people inoculate themselves from the ugliness by declining to engage in anything uncomfortable? How many build walls of isolation for the purpose of keeping away reality about the world and the darkness that often makes it go around? How many don't engage and offer their gifts to God as a solution to the pain in the world because it's too hard to *know*?

The Church is not a building. The Church is a body of believers, followers of Jesus Christ—people—united for the glory of God. For the Church to be the Church, we have to take it outside to where the suffering is, where God is, but people don't see him. We have to go and point to him in the darkest places. We have to be willing to look at the bad.

The Ugly

There are times when the Church has been and still is persecuted. [6]And there are times when people have suffered persecution from people that call themselves "the Church."

Certain groups and factions have carried out their own hate-filled actions in the guise of fulfilling their Christian duty. Devastation has come at the hands of people who uphold misogynistic, racist, and classist ideology. The bottom line is that people that call themselves "the Church" have found themselves on the right and wrong side of history at various times. And we cannot ignore that. We cannot skip the parts of history that are not favorable to us or our narrative, the ugly parts.

Try talking to an unbeliever about faith in Jesus. Are you ready to answer for the Crusades, the Inquisition, Catholics burning Protestants, then Protestants burning Catholics, then witches? Are you ready to answer for Evangelicalism's opposition to racial integration? How about slavery? The list goes on, and we should be ready to answer for it. We serve a perfect Savior who loves an imperfect and always evolving Bride. What should never change is our fealty to our Lord and Savior (who remains the same), but what must always change is our prejudices, racism, and close-mindedness about things to which Jesus is open.

Sometimes our checkered past immobilizes us and keeps us from moving forward. Just like the individual who lives with shame about his past sins, whole cultures can become para-

---

6   "The 50 Countries Where It's Most Dangerous to Follow Jesus in 2021," *Christianity Today*, January 13, 2021. https://www.christianitytoday.com/news/2021/january/christian-persecution-2021-countries-open-doors-watch-list.html.

lyzed in their collective shame. Always be looking and listening to the ugliness of the past and the present. Always ask yourself: What aspects of this situation am I not familiar with based on my lived experience? Where might I be blind? What are "they" saying that I don't understand? Ask and be open to learn and act according to God's commands.

Are diversity, equity, and inclusion just a state of being, or are there material and spiritual benefits to this kind of worldview, mindset, and Church culture? Are more souls discipled when believers and churches operate with an inclusive mindset/culture? Will the body of Christ grow faster? Perhaps homogenous church growth is more effective with man-centered numerical growth, but Christ-centered spiritual growth requires prayer and intention.

Does the impact of the ministry become more dynamic? Just think about it for a moment. Maybe you have spent your whole life in a bubble. Maybe you have stayed in your church in your denomination, unwilling to consider what other followers of Jesus Christ are doing and thinking about—either unwilling or just blissfully unaware. But as God would have it, you are reading this book. You are moving Godward with eternity in mind.

There will be greater trust from the communities that the Church is called to serve when we get serious about following Christ's example for ministry to the lost. One pastor and church planter I know, who happens to be a white, middle-aged male, is candid about the temptation and struggle when it comes to church growth, especially in a new church. Reaching the lost, especially the lost among diverse groups, can be extraordinarily difficult. First, Satan opposes it and will use every trick in the book to ruin it. Second, most of the time, like 99 percent of it, a person doesn't move from total nonbeliever uninterested in Jesus and church to a full-fledged serving, giving, helping member in a very short time. The lost are only low hanging fruit during a time of miraculous revival.

I pray we are due for just such a revival. Let us pray fervently that God will send revival to our city, our country, and our world. God does a great work and people repent. He knows it all and will one day return for his diverse Bride. The question for you and me is: Will we be building when he comes? Will there be oil in our lamps? We will be praying, acting, and working?

> "Blessed is that servant whom his master will find so doing when he comes" (Mt 24:46 ESV).

CHAPTER EIGHT:

Move Beyond Lip Service

So many people today are "talking." Virtue signaling is at an all-time high as social media is on fire with people rushing to "action." By *action*, I mean performative, trending, superficial statements. People seem to think that once they have made a Twitter post affirming the side they're on, they've done something. But for actual change to occur, we must be ready to move beyond lip service. Talking is a good first start, but as they say, *talk is cheap*.

Lead in Word *and* Deed

> "Dear children, let us not love with words or speech but with actions and in truth" (1 Jn 3:18 NIV).

> "My little children, let us not love in word, neither in tongue; but in deed and in truth" (KJV).

Deeds equal actions. I'll be transparent and vulnerable. At first, I wrestled with God about writing this book. I tried Moses' "not me" approach when God started calling me to action. When God told Moses to go back to Egypt and tell Pharoah to let his people go, Moses protested. He thought God must not have thought it through.

Exodus 4:10 says,

> But Moses pleaded with the LORD, "O Lord, I'm not very good with words. I never have been, and I'm not now, even though you have spoken to me. I get tongue-tied, and my words get tangled." (NLT)

I rattled off the stereotypical mantras around gender, race, and age as reasons why someone else would be better suited to bring this message to the world. I was discouraged until I realized that these negative thoughts were not my thoughts. Instead, they were planted as seeds by the media and individuals who want to uphold the status quo for which voices are heard or muted.

So, I put on my big girl pants and sought seasoned godly counsel concerning how to share this message with integrity and biblical truth. It was no longer enough for me to just talk about these issues with my friends, family, and fellow believers in a bubble. It was time to move beyond lip service to meaningful action. I found peace by remembering that this is a part of God's model for inclusion, and he will provide the resources needed to accomplish his will.

We send messages by our actions more than our words. We send messages by who we promote to leadership roles, whose voice is amplified, and whose voice is muted. These messages impact a person's perception of themselves. Look around your church, your ministries, your home. What messages are you sending? There are intended and unintended consequences for our actions and the messages we convey. This is why Christ-centered action is so powerful and critical.

Look at biblical examples for how God chose leaders, how Christ chose disciples, and who Christ interacted with regardless of societal norms. What patterns do you see? Christ has thankfully given us our best example of what it looks like to move beyond words to actions. Jesus was the Word of God wrapped in flesh—the living Word (Jn 1:14). How can we become the living Word? What specific actions will demonstrate that the Word of God is alive in us?

The Fruits of the Spirit
Galatians 5:22 says,

> "But the fruit of the Spirit is love, joy, peace, patience, kindness, goodness, faithfulness, gentleness, self-control; against such things there is no law" (NASB).

A biblical way of saying, "take action" is "bear fruit." The fruit of the Spirit refers both to a way of being, and a way of action. Love is a noun, but it is also a verb. We are called to *be* loving, and to love others (see Chapter 5). Let's consider the other "fruits of the Spirit" as they pertain to ways of both acting and being, and let's apply it specifically to God's heart for diversity, equity, and inclusion.

Joy

There has been much discussion about the difference between joy and happiness. Happiness could be defined as a momentary response to external stimuli. Happiness is fleeting, coming and going depending on our circumstances. Happiness can be taken from us in a heartbeat when we experience something sad, challenging, or maddening. Happiness, by this definition, is part of our chemical wiring, as is sadness.

Biblical joy is different. Happiness is not a fruit of the Holy Spirit, but joy is. Joy is something deep within us that doesn't change with our fleeting emotions. Joy is a gift from God that is continually with us and guides our lives. Joy characterizes the children of God and makes them evident. Why? Because through our faith, we know that *nothing* could ever separate us from the love of God. No matter what we face in life, everything will be ok because we know our eternal destiny is secure in Christ.

So, what does joy have to do with DEI? To truly live out a godly and loving vision of DEI, one must be rooted in joy. God's love and joy in our hearts go hand in hand. When we are living and walking in God's love, joy is the natural result within us. And we will live out true DEI when we are acting as representatives of Christ and reflecting God's love to everyone in this beautifully diverse world around us.

We can do hard things when we act for our joy. Christ died on the cross, we are told, "for the *joy* set before him" (Heb 12:2 NIV). Joy can move us to do great things. The promise of joy when we *act* in obedience to God's will, is more than enough to cause us to walk whatever hard road is before us.

Peace and Patience

Next are peace and patience, which naturally flow into each other. To be patient, your heart must be in a place of peace. A restless or discontent heart will not be nearly as patient as one that is rooted in the peace only God can provide.

And what is this peace that God provides? How is it different from what we find in the world around us? This peace is not tied to fleeting, momentary things like financial security or human relationships. The peace God pours into our hearts is rooted in his eternal, all-encompassing, and fervent love. We have peace because we know that we are children of the almighty God and that Christ has already won the victory for us on the cross. We also have peace when we are walking according to his will for us.

This peace helps to shape our hearts, allowing us to slow down and emulate Christ, looking toward the needs of others before our own. When we can do that, we are able to empathize with people in ways we couldn't otherwise. Sometimes we are so blinded by our wants and needs that it's hard to be patient with others. But that's because we are being pulled in the wrong direction by our human, worldly nature. When we instead live by the ways of Christ and the Holy Spirit, we are able to see past that and truly strive to serve the other person instead. Walking in the Spirit brings us a peace that passes understanding and along with it, the patience to trust in God's plan against our human desires. For positive action toward DEI, this is exactly what is required.

Kindness, Goodness, and Faithfulness

Kindness, goodness, and faithfulness all work into DEI as well. Kindness is simple. Just think of the golden rule: treat other people the way you'd like to be treated. Treat people with godly love, dignity, and respect. If you need inspiration, just look toward the example of Jesus in the Bible. Look at how he treats people—always with kindness. He also tested people's faith at times and pushed them to go deeper in their belief in him as their savior. Even when he showed "tough love," it was always with the best intentions to bring about a positive godly outcome.

Goodness is similar to kindness but speaks more to the beliefs, morals, and motivations that inspire our actions. We were created in God's image, and goodness is our gift from him. He is good in every way and always acts in goodness toward everyone. Being created in his image, we are made to do the same. Our kind acts toward others are a way we express the goodness of God that he has placed within us.

And there is faithfulness. Faithfulness means that we always act in the best interest of others and our relationship with them following Christ's example. When we are faithful to another, we never act in a way that would demean them, hurt our relationship, or sabotage the trust between us. Additionally, faithfulness is what we will employ when our work and relationships require us to hang on through the troubles that may come our way as we engage. DEI can be hard work. Remember, Jesus only had twelve members to look after and look at all he went through—and he is God.

Gentleness

Another fruit from the Holy Spirit that determines how we interact and treat others is gentleness. When we express gentleness toward them, we act in a loving way despite the circumstances. Even if we need to have a hard or challenging conversation with someone, we do it out of a place of respect and love. When we live out gentleness as a fruit of the Spirit, it means that we express that gentleness to everyone, no matter who they are or where they're from.

It's saddening to hear name calling and insults hurled around carelessly, especially in the body of Christ. We must model gentleness even when we have righteous anger. I ask you to pause and think calmly about this question. How effective is a ministry that insults individuals or groups and then makes an invitation for salvation? Or an invitation to join their faith community?

Colossians 4:6 says,

> "Let your conversation be always full of grace, seasoned with salt, so that you may know how to answer everyone" (NIV).

Self-Control

Self-control is essential for every child of God. No matter how closely we walk with God or how committed we are to walking a godly path, we all make mistakes and feel urges we don't want to feel. Self-control is the ability to draw strength from our faith and do what we know is right even when we don't particularly feel like it. There will be times when, encountering someone different than us in some way, our first instinct won't be to respond in a positive way. But when we work on our self-control, we will be able to process our feelings and respond in a godly manner.

Another way to think about self-control is through the lens of stewardship. An essential part of being human is being a steward, a manager of God's property. In the parable of the talents, each servant is given a measure of talents, that is, money to manage on behalf of the master who promises to return and demand an account. It can be tempting to identify with the servant of only one or two talents and simply compare ourselves to those who seem to have been given more.

But this is a mistake because stewardship is a powerful principle, and everyone has been given what they need to grow their talents exponentially for an eternity—partially on earth and partially in Heaven and the new heavens and earth to come ("Come share your master's happiness" (Mt 25:24 NIV; "Take charge of ten cities" (Lk 25:24 NIV)).

What has this to do with self-control? Because you have at least one talent to start with. Yourself. Your mind, time, and energy. You decide what to do. Will you bury it in the yard? Or will you make the most of it? The principle of stewardship means that life works by spirals. You can spiral up, or you can spiral down. You need to take a first step in the upward direction. You can help others up. You can push others down. What spiritual fruit is required for this? *Self-control.*

Call it self-management, self-stewardship, ownership, taking responsibility. You have no idea just what a powerful concept this is. Exercise self-control to exercise all the other fruits! This is the essence of "moving beyond lip service." We decide. We choose to take biblical action and bear fruit.

Be the Church

My grandmother, Mildred Little, says, "You are not a church-goer. You are the Church." Church is not somewhere you go, it's who you are and what you do. If we are going to lead in this conversation, we need to practice the fruit of the Spirit. We also need to remember that we are the Church, and if we are the Church, there are some things we need to get right, including the following:

- Christian is not synonymous with conservative or liberal. People often make broad generalizations about political affiliations. *Conservatives love life for the unborn, and freedom, and moral justice. Progressives love to care for the poor, inclusion of everyone, and mercy.* Guess what? Jesus loves all those things!

- The Church should always engage in civil discourse with a voice of hope and love.

- The current state of division in America offers an opportunity for the Church to model the fruit of the Spirit. Rather than look at the moral decay and division as a sign that the enemy has won, let's look at it as an opportunity for living our purpose in Christ. Church history has some blights on it, but it also has bright spots. When the plague ravaged the earth, it was the Church who stood out for caring for the sick, dying, and heartbroken, even at the cost of their own lives. As a result, the Church grew exponentially in those times. We have another opportunity for global compassion and discipleship now.

- Some of the complex issues we face will not be answered until we are in Heaven. I don't have all of the answers to life's hard questions. No one does. But that is not an excuse to not address the issues that we do have answers to with integrity, passion, generosity, and charity.

- We can co-create a path forward, or *Godward*, in solidarity without finger-pointing blame or shame. We can find common ground with those who we disagree with by staying focused on winning souls for Christ. We can gather for face-to-face conversations to cut off a major weapon of the enemy, isolation. Rather than sending a text or ping from our electronic devices, we can share meals and fellowship. We can seek to understand one another's perspectives and celebrate the sovereignty of God's diverse creation.

- We can remember that unlike privilege—a byproduct of the social constructs of race and money—salvation truly is universally accessible and available for all. We can follow the example of Jesus, who absolutely scandalized the establishment by going to the very ones who had been denied access.

- We can help believers, churches, missionaries, and outreach groups avoid the traps of voluntourism, savior complex, and modern colonization. We can pray and discern what kinds of outreach knock down dividing walls and what kinds build them up. So many ways we've tried to do this have created the dreaded and unhelpful "us vs. them" mentality. We can't just give to the poor, we must understand that we are all the poor and live among one another in reciprocal relationships where each party adds and accepts value.

In order to move beyond lip service, we may just have to realize that many times we don't know what we're doing, and we must trust the Holy Spirit's leading. We may not be able to wait until we have a perfect grand plan. Just pray, educate yourself, step out of the house, and go love someone who you would normally not have interacted with because of your differences. Just do it with the right motive and leave room for God to make all things work together for good.

CHAPTER NINE:

Make Room for Controversy and Conflict

Love is the answer. What's the question?

When my son graduated college, he came out as queer. Being queer is defined as non-binary or any other orientation than straight. There was chaos swirling around me from gossiping family, friends, and fellow believers. Everyone had an opinion about what I should do. Christian counsel offered generic advice like, "you just need to pray and trust God." While the situation was overwhelming, I was not confused about how I needed to respond to my son when he came out. I reassured him that I will always love him. I spoke to him as I always had about God having a plan for his life and that he is created to be a mighty man of valor. I will always pray for him and call forth the God-given greatness in him until God calls me home.

My love response for my son did not go over well with my zealous family and friends. I remember thinking, "Do these people really believe I should turn my back on my son? I'd die for him." And quite frankly, anyone who ever bothered my son would be in for some pretty severe consequences from me. That's the most Christian way my Southern-born and raised self can express my response to anyone that dared to mess with my first-born precious child.

I also said to myself, I've prayed with some of these people when their daughters became pregnant out of wedlock, their sons were admitted to rehab or incarcerated, their spouses had affairs, and more. Now they wanted to shun me and tell me to turn on my son. I was livid.

But this highlights the great controversy. How should we respond to the sins that so many place at the top of their list as the worst transgression? While I have more questions than answers relative to these complex issues, I sincerely believe based on the way Christ responded to sinners—the answer is love. To put it frankly, *You should respond the same way you want Christ to respond to the sin in your life.*

This ongoing reality of my own life and experience is one of the many reasons I refuse to check a box. I will never compromise my faith for my son, popular thinking, public opinion, or a political party line agenda. And I will never turn my back on my son for friends, family, a political agenda, or a false narrative of sin ranking.

The world is full of sin. How should we respond as the body of Christ? With love. God knew the path of man before he created Adam. He also prepared the way for salvation. "For God so **loved** the world that **he gave** his one and only Son, so that **whosoever** would believe in him would not perish but have eternal life" (Jn 3:16 NIV emphasis added).

Whosoever means whosoever. We don't get to classify and rank sin based on our own bias toward certain behaviors or lifestyles. Sin is sin and the Bible says "all have sinned." So how should we respond? I know some people like to debate the couple places in the Bible that seem to indicate that some sin is worse than others or that some may be punished more harshly than others.

> I tell you, on the day of judgment people will give account for every careless word they speak, for by your words you will be justified, and by your words you will be condemned. (Mt. 12:36–37 ESV)

And this one:

> How much worse punishment, do you think, will be deserved by the one who has trampled underfoot the Son of God, and has profaned the blood of the covenant by which he was sanctified, and has outraged the Spirit of grace? (Heb. 10:29 ESV)

These verses seem to indicate that any degrees of punishment come not from what kinds of sin, but rather how much sin and relative to how much revelation has been given. "To whom much is given, much is required" (Lk 12:48).

That said, I've tried my best to stay in my lane as the facilitator of this conversation and leave it to you to exegete these

Scriptures with your pastor and your local leadership. I'm also tempted to bring in some hermeneutics and apologetics, but that is not my assignment for this book. My personal conviction is that I do not want to get caught up in how much sin or which sins will keep me out of Heaven.

As a result, I choose to follow the biblical principles outlined by Paul in 1 Corinthians 15:31. "I assure you, believers, by the pride which I have in you in [your union with] Christ Jesus our Lord, I die daily [I face death and die to self]" (AMP). Meditating on this Scripture helps to keep us humble and grounded in the fact that tomorrow is not promised to anyone. It's also a great reminder that we need to die daily to any sin in our lives regardless of what "rank" we assign to it.

All of these considerations contribute to the fundamental understanding that we are not honoring God if we turn our backs on our loved ones because they sin differently from us. It does mean that we speak the truth in love about their sin—and ours. I don't tell my son that I think it's great and that he is living according to God's plan. I tell my son I love him. I'm here for him, and I always will be. He has his own relationship with God to deal with, and I will walk beside him through it all.

One reason for the lack of diversity in the Church, and also the lack of effectiveness toward reaching lost people in the world, is our unwillingness to love and welcome people as they are. If Christ's prerequisite for salvation was that we had to be perfect and without sin—no one would ever be saved.

We as the Church have been self-righteous and religious, making a list of which sins are okay for church members to be constantly committing (gluttony) and which sins are not. What has happened is that in our own sin, we have compromised. We have allowed ourselves to get away with the sins that we are simply unable to abstain from. We have struggled to deal with this, and part of the way we have accepted our own weakness is to judge those in the world who struggle where we don't and call their sin worse than ours.

Or even worse, they struggle with the same sins we do. How many times has a prominent pastor or Christian personality harshly condemned people who commit certain sins, only for it to come out later that they have been living a lie and committing those same sins all along. You can probably think of several. This proves that much of the hatred for "sinners" is really out of self-hatred.

So, what then is God's heart for the sinner? How does God look at anyone who is living in any sort of habitual sin? The first example that comes to mind is the Prodigal Son found in Luke 15:11–32. I'll paraphrase it here. A man has two sons and the youngest says to his father, "Give me my inheritance so I can go into the world." Incredibly, the father gives it to him. The son takes the money and then leaves to a far country where he squanders it all on revelry. His life falls apart, especially when a famine comes.

It is right to say that those who have fallen into a life of sin have turned away from God. Our response depends on how closely we want to follow Christ's example. Many will jump at the chance to judge and condemn. They focus on how the prodigal son dishonored and hurt his father, took his inheritance, and wasted it all on temporal pleasures. They also focus on how he, as we all do, tried to do things his own way and ended up failing.

Conversely, I propose we prayerfully seize these opportunities to love, evangelize, and disciple. We need to remind ourselves of our fallen state prior to us accepting the gift of salvation. It's from this precipice that we can delve even deeper into the mystery of God's response to sin versus man's response.

While this story is horribly sad for the prodigal son; it ends well because he has a loving father. God shows his heart for the lost sinner by the actions of the father in this parable. He doesn't condemn the son in his life's choices. He simply loves, prays, and waits for him to return. It's worth noting that the father's response is vastly different from the other brother. We will take a look at the other brother's actions as well, but first the father.

The Father
Jesus describes the father as though he is out in the fields, perhaps on a high lookout watching the horizon. Maybe he heard about the famine in the country where his son had gone. We learn that the son's idea was to go home and offer himself as a servant in his father's house. He considered himself unworthy to come back as a son, but he knew his father's servants ate well and had a roof over their heads.

The father sees his son on the horizon. He knows his son has made mistakes. He knows he will be coming home in shame. Perhaps he knows that the norm would have been to wait for his son to come and bow down at his feet, begging. But that is not what the father did. He did not care that the son had made mistakes. He only cared about one thing. This son " was dead and is alive again; he was lost and is found" (Lk 15:32 NIV).

People who are newly saved read this differently than those who have been saved awhile. When the acceptance and love of Jesus is fresh in your life, it is easy to relate to the younger son and be amazed and joyful at the thought. God forgives the very worst of sinners. Jesus extended love to those who the society, especially the religious establishment, had given up on. Not only had society given up on them, society blamed them. God was judging Israel because of these sinners.

The Brother

Those of us who have followed Jesus for a while often find ourselves drifting to the side of the older brother. "Hey, why should they get mercy? We've been here all along!" But the older brother is mistaken about something crucial. He is presented as someone who feels betrayed by his father's acceptance of the returning prodigal. He seems to think that the prodigal has gotten away with something. He thinks his brother was somehow having a "good time" and is now being rewarded for it.

Jesus specifically told this story to the Jews because he saw that they didn't understand God's grace, God's love, God's plan, or God's heart for the prodigals. We must allow God to give us his heart for the prodigal. It starts with empathy. If you spent much time as a prodigal, you may remember the hell you were in. You may remember the fear, insecurity, the dishonesty and lies, the depravity of trying to gratify an insatiable desire for meaning, for pleasure, for something, anything that would alleviate a fear of death, abandonment, and rejection.

We can rejoice when someone sees the light and returns from such a lifestyle. Even better, we can stand on the hilltop with the father and watch for those coming home. We are spiritually mature when we meet people out in the world and love them unconditionally, bless them, pray for them, do good to them. We can even bless our persecutors.

Caught in Adultery

One other example of Christ's love is the story of the woman caught in adultery. I'll highlight it here from ESV.

> But Jesus went to the Mount of Olives. Early in the morning he came again to the temple. All the people came to him, and he sat down and taught them. The scribes and the Pharisees brought a woman who had been caught in adultery, and placing her in the midst they said to him, "Teacher, this woman has been caught in the act of adultery. Now in the Law, Moses commanded us to stone such women. So what do you say?" This they said to test him, that they might have some charge to bring against him. Jesus bent down and wrote with his finger on the ground. And as they continued to ask him, he stood up and said to them, "Let him who is without sin among you be the first to throw a stone at her." And once more he bent down and wrote on the ground. But when they heard it, they went away one by one, beginning with the older ones, and Jesus was left alone with the woman standing before him. Jesus stood up and said to her, "Woman, where are they? Has no one condemned you?" She said, "No one, Lord." And Jesus said, "Neither do I condemn you; go, and from now on sin no more. (Jn 8:1–11)

The Jews simply wanted to kill her, but they wanted to test Jesus first. They had suspected he was more merciful than was appropriate, that he didn't take God's law as seriously as they did, so they brought her and wanted to see what he would say and do. They thought they could trap him. "What do you say?"

"Let him who is without sin among you cast the first stone." Remarkably, the oldest ones dropped their stones and walked away, and the younger ones followed. Jesus said to the woman then, "I don't condemn you; go, and from now on sin no more."

We don't know what she did after that, but the story paints a perfect picture of grace, forgiveness, and the transformation that comes as a result. We came to God deserving death for our sins. Jesus does not condemn us but forgives, telling us to change. This is called repentance, and anyone is invited to come and repent of sins and change, to lay down the life of running from God and take up an abundant and blessed life of running to him and with him.

Both stories, the prodigal and the adulterer, show us the heart we are to have for those far away from God. In this way, we "make room for controversy and conflict." Older brothers and Pharisees will not like it when God's arms open for people who they blame for society's ills.

And it is not just "sinners" that some people have trouble accepting. Sometimes, people don't want to associate with people that worship differently, prefer loud praise church services, dance in church, or speak in tongues. The real question is how to have a Christ-centered response to differences that make us uncomfortable. In short, if we aren't navigating some controversy and conflict, we likely are not practicing God's model for inclusion.

If we are going to "make room for controversy and conflict," then we must adopt a radically generous attitude towards those who are not exactly like us or think like us on all issues, especially the controversial ones. The only way to do that is through the power of the Holy Spirit. Jesus told us to love our brothers and sisters, our neighbor, and our enemies. Who is left off of this list? No one. If someone's views upset you, you can still love them. Even as you engage them in debate, you can be set free of hatred. Is your hatred brought on by fear? Is your anger righteous? If so, then respond in righteousness. Ask yourself this question honestly. Ask God and he will show you. Why are you afraid to love others who are and think differently than you?

The following came from a website of The Latter Day Saints:[7] Some people may not be able to accept the sound principles in this concept because of their opinions about Mormons and their own beliefs. Regardless of what some people may think, this article was spot on.

> True sons and daughters of God test their love against the "even if" list. For example–
>
> I will love you even if you ... lie.
>
> I will love you even if you ... steal.
>
> I will love you even if you ... yell at me.
>
> I will love you even if you ... abandon your covenants.

---

7   Larry Barkdull, "A Crucial Lesson from the Brother of the Prodigal Son." *Meridian Magazine*, January 27, 2019, https://latterdaysaintmag.com/a-crucial-lesson-from-the-brother-of-the-prodigal-son/)

> I will love you even if you ... drink, smoke, take drugs.
>
> I will love you even if you ... commit sexual sin.
>
> I will love you even if you ... choose an alternative lifestyle.
>
> I will love you even if you ... leave home and don't talk with me for years.
>
> I will love you even if you ... betray me.
>
> I will love you even if you ... are committed to prison.
>
> I will love you even if you ... have an abortion.
>
> We might ask ourselves: At what point would my love cease? Where we would judge, does God's love cease? One of the exacting prices of becoming like God is to learn to love "even if."

Many people would look at this list and think, "Sure, no problem," but if the loved one has a different opinion about politics, we're not able to even have a conversation. This is tragic, and it falls into Satan's trap for believers.

A pastor friend was leading a fairly diverse church in St. Louis, MO when Michael Brown was shot by police officer Darren Wilson. The issue tore the church apart. The pastor, a white man, describes how at every turn, his attempts to address the situation received incredible push back from one side or another. Trying to stay "in the middle" and keep everyone together, he failed on all fronts. What had been a church with an 80:20 white to Black ratio, ended the year 99:1 white to Black. There were also white police officers who left the church in that time.

But there was one, and only one, bright spot. In hindsight they did one thing right on the advice of another pastor, a Black man, who led a diverse church with closer to a 50/50 split. That man told him to have a forum where they would not debate what happened but would discuss race in general. The two questions that all participants had the opportunity to answer were:

1. When did you first understand race as a category?
2. When did you first witness racism?

The answers ranged from Black youths feeling out of place at their majority white high school to an older woman witnessing a lynching and being kicked out of the "whites only" section of a restaurant. There was also a white police officer who admitted to profiling in traffic stops. The shocking result was that everyone felt heard, felt connected to the "others" in the room, and felt hope for a world, or at least a Church, that could be a peaceful place for diversity and disagreement.

Unfortunately, this happened only once, which was a good start but not enough. This should have taken place regularly for a year, or even forever. But the pastor learned a powerful lesson for the future. Satan cannot call the shots when we are willing to get together and seek to learn from one another. This requires that we do not fear conflict and controversy, but trust God to guide us through it. In fact, if you don't have conflict and controversy in your church, then it is 99 percent likely that you "enjoy" a monoculture.

Here is my practical advice for how to respond to controversial situations and conflicts as a believer: Always try to call people in. Never call people out. Call out specific behaviors and address them accordingly, but always try to call the person in. Always try to call people into fellowship with other believers and into a relationship with Jesus Christ. Pray about what to say or do in touchy situations.

Jesus's disciples, both before and after the resurrection, are the example for a diverse, equitable, and inclusive church. Jesus chose to closely associate with people from all walks of life. Many times he interacted with people that "the Church" shunned. At Pentecost, the Holy Spirit was poured out on a Church that has rarely reached a greater level of diversity since.

The Bible provides countless examples of diversity, equity, and inclusion. What are yours? In your everyday lived experiences what can/should you do?

Simply said, treat people the way God invites us to in the Bible. Show how your life's examples match the Bible's interpretation and *make room for conflict and controversy*. God can handle it, and so can a true faith.

CHAPTER TEN:

Invite New Perspectives

In the last chapter, I talked about my friend's church experience in St. Louis after the events that took place in Ferguson. When everyone got together and spoke about their experiences with racism, it worked because they were able to invite new perspectives. Each of us has our own experiences, biases, assumptions, and values, and most of us don't enjoy having those challenged. We pick the talk radio that we agree with, and we hang out with "our people" and reinforce our dearly held perspectives. This feels good, safe, and secure. We feel bonded with our own community and enjoy strength in numbers. We even enjoy fighting a common enemy on the "other side."

But of course, this perpetuates the problem of disunity and every evil that comes with it.

I shared my testimony of God's miraculous healing power in my book, *You Are Still Good*.[8] I described how my daughter suffered a stroke at the age of seventeen. I've noticed several

---

8   La'Wana Harris, *You Are Still Good: A Mother's Testimony of Faith and Prayer* (La'Wana Harris, 2017).

recurring questions each time I share with a new group. "Why did you drive your daughter to the hospital instead of calling 911?" In public, I usually respond saying I knew I needed to get her to the hospital as quickly as possible. This is a true statement, but I want to share the deeper truth behind my actions with you.

There is a sentiment among the Black community that 911 response times are slower in predominantly Black lower income neighborhoods. I'd heard this repeated throughout my entire life including in church. I did not even hesitate it or debate it in my mind. I knew with every part of me they wouldn't come in time, so I drove her.

I've also heard and read that Black women are much more likely to be underdiagnosed and not treated for serious acute illnesses. So when I got to the hospital with my daughter, and the nurse kept telling me to have a seat, I was *completely triggered* because I knew from my own medical training and my pure mother's instinct that something was seriously wrong with my daughter and that time was critical.

I had to fight to get them to give her urgent care. "This is my daughter, and I know something serious is going on!" I insisted. A nurse finally and reluctantly checked Jasmine's blood pressure, and it was as if all the blood rushed out of her face. She immediately ran to call a code that summoned an army of nurses and doctors into the room. By this time, Jasmine was completely nonresponsive. They put her on an IV, and once she was stabilized, they took her for a CAT scan. She had a massive blood clot and also a bleed in her brain.

After the doctors delivered the poor prognosis that my child would die, they sent me to "the little quiet room" and the hospital chaplain came to ask me if I needed anything. I promptly responded, "Yes, can you print me some healing Scriptures?" The look of bewilderment on the chaplain's face still baffles me. It was as though he didn't know such Scriptures existed. As followers in Jesus Christ, we have an opportunity to share hope and faith in times of despair. In fairness, I guess he did not want to get my hopes up seeing that the doctors all but said my daughter was going to die, but what I needed was a man or woman of faith at that moment. I needed someone open to another viewpoint about the situation.

Now let's parse this out a bit. What if the intake nurse had invited a *new perspective* on why some Black people and communities of color tend to bring their loved ones to the hospital instead of calling 911? Could she have done a better job triaging our emergency? Could she have avoided her false assumption that someone who walks in the hospital or is wheeled in by a family member is not to automatically be considered as being in a less critical condition?

When we know better, we can do better.

I share this story, specifically, because I consider the local church to be a hospital of sorts. People come to church broken, hurt, battered, and bruised. They may show up just after a domestic dispute, a painful divorce, or just after being released from rehab or prison.

Are you part of a "come as you are" church or a "get in where you fit in" church? We have an awesome opportunity and responsibility to shepherd and disciple the people that come to our ministry. How can we be sure that our faith community is a safe and welcoming place for everyone?

Are we worshiping in a bubble? How can we open ourselves up to better understand the people we are called to serve? And who exactly are we called to serve? Do we see our missional calling as looking for the people who we are most comfortable with? To be fair, this was taught as a strategy for reaching people for a long time. It does make some sense. After all, you can best understand the people who are just like you. They will identify best with you. They will trust you more easily and quickly.

The homogenous unit principle has been used to grow massive congregations across America, if not the world. But this has done a lot of damage to the cause of unity and the demolition of "dividing walls of hostility." In short, building monocultures and echo chambers of people who are similar in every way is something that can be done on a purely human level. How do we know these Christian communities are of God when the unity is so psychological?

I'm not saying that nothing good ever happens in churches where everyone is the same, but I am saying that something very powerful occurs when we allow God to build our churches in a way that reflects the Kingdom of Heaven. In these churches, part of the discipleship journey is being challenged on your perspectives. Listening to other peoples' experiences and opinions opens your own mind to things you've never considered or had to consider before.

Openness and Curiosity

The truth is that openness is a personality trait that psychologists can measure on tests such as the [9]Big Five Personalities Test. When you are high in trait openness, you actually like hearing other perspectives because you get easily bored with just one perspective. You're the person who is always into something new. You are generally an interesting person because you tend to know a little about a lot and can converse on many topics on many levels. Hearing other perspectives doesn't threaten you but rather stimulates your thinking.

As far as anyone has been able to tell, the average person taking the test scores at an average level of openness, with minorities on either extreme. A highly open person, or open-minded person, will thrive in a diverse ministry environment where new perspectives are invited. But even the average person is not naturally open enough to gravitate to that. The majority of people simply want to be comfortable and do not like to be challenged.

But consider our faith. Was it not started by people who were willing to follow Jesus? Wasn't Jesus every bit the opposite of the status quo? Isn't that why they crucified him?

According to experts who measure this trait in people, there are ways to increase your curiosity and openness to new experiences and perspectives.[10]

---

9   (n.d.). *The Big Five Personality Test*. Truity. https://www.truity.com/test/big-five-personality-test

10   "Openness to Experience: Meaning, Examples & How to Improve Your Openness," HIGH5 TEST, accessed February 23, 2022, https://high5test.com/openness-to-experience/.

First, give up being self-absorbed. Humans are obsessed with themselves. It's true that you must practice self-care and consider yourself and how you are living your life. It's true that responsibility for yourself is a basic starting point for stewardship. But *self-absorption* is different. It is constantly thinking about yourself in terms of evaluating through the eyes of others. Especially for those who do not know God, this can be a full-time job. We are obsessed with monitoring our status, our looks, our importance. It's exhausting, and it closes us off to inviting new perspectives.

But God says, "Do nothing from selfish ambition or conceit, but in humility count others more significant than yourselves" (Phil 2:3 ESV). Another way to say this would be, *Give yourself a break from navel gazing and self-obsession. You have permission to focus outside yourself in a gloriously free way.* Self-absorption is bondage. Focusing on others is freedom. If this is something you struggle with, go to God and ask him to help you surrender it. He will help those who ask. When you stop focusing on yourself, you will become more open to new perspectives.

The second way to become more open is related to the first, get your identity squarely rooted in Christ. If you know who you are, a child of God, then you don't have to feel threatened when other people don't agree with you. The idea of changing your mind as a result of someone's good argument doesn't have to terrify you. Who are you? You are an image-bearer of the Creator. You are a brand-new creation in Christ, a vessel of the Holy Spirit and a child of God who is awaiting an imperishable inheritance with him for an eternity. You can handle hearing other perspectives. You don't have to believe them or adopt them unless you find them to be true, in which case you have grown in wisdom and knowledge!

The third thing is to travel the world (live or virtual) or at least find some way to step outside your bubble of comfort. Traveling and exploring other cultures will show you how God's plan for diversity and inclusion is perfect. Your own bubble can feel enormous. The happenings and people that populate your world seem all-encompassing to you, and all the while there are billions of people outside your bubble living lives in their own comfort zones. Go see why they do what they do and believe what they believe. Test it against your own beliefs and ways. If your ways are right, you will reinforce your beliefs about them. If they are not, you will be able to discard falsehoods or mistakes.

Fourth, simply invite someone who you know is different from you in some area to have a conversation. Make a commitment and do it. Commit to listening to them and being able to reflect back their point of view until they agree you are hearing them accurately. Try not to project your own personality or motive on them. Often we will judge someone's reasons as though they had our own traumas and issues. We think, "If I thought that, here's why I would." But realize that may not be the case at all.

Fifth, try new things. Especially if you are used to living a certain way, eating certain foods, engaging in certain pastimes, try something completely different. Take a class, study a subject, join a club of some kind. Commit to trying this for six months. It will open your world up to other ideas and kinds of people. Break your routine whenever you can. Take a different commute for a while. Dress a bit differently than you normally would. Eat differently. Try stuff out.

Finally, we can grow exponentially in the area of openness if we recapture the art of talking to strangers. Joe Keohane, the author of *The Power of Strangers: The Benefits of Connecting in a Suspicious World*, makes an entertaining, yet powerful case for reengaging in this lost art.[11] In an article he wrote about the topic for Entrepreneur.com, he describes taking a class from Georgie Nightingall that discussed her company, Trigger Conversations in London, that helps people learn to have better human connections.[12] Keohane writes,

---

11   Joe Keohane, *The Power of Strangers: The Benefits of Connecting in a Suspicious World* (New York, Random House, 2021.)
12   Joe Keohane, "How to Become a Master at Talking to Strangers." *Entrepreneur*, July 7, 2021, https://www.entrepreneur.com/starting-a-business/how-to-become-a-master-at-talking-to-strangers/375641.

> Nightingall has learned that, for a lot of people, the hardest thing about talking to strangers is initiating the conversation: approaching someone, making them feel safe, and quickly conveying the idea that you don't have an agenda, that you're just being friendly or curious. She found that older people are much more likely to initiate a conversation, for instance, whereas younger people require a little more assurance. But she also found that in all her own attempts to speak to strangers, the vast majority of those interactions were substantial, and many went great.
>
> She came to believe, too — and this is important — that making a practice of talking to strangers could offer more than a jolt of good feeling for an individual. There was joy in it, profundity, real communion. If practiced widely enough, she believed it could help repair a fracturing society. "We're not just talking about a few individualized things," she says. "We're talking about a different way to live."

"If practiced widely enough, she believed it could help repair a fracturing society." That's exactly what we're talking about in this book. My immediate goal would be for you, the reader, to become more open to diversity, equity, and inclusion. Zooming out one level, it would be that your church would benefit by your new openness and that it could become more of a reflection of the global Kingdom of God. But the ultimate goal for all of it would be to "help repair a fracturing society!" This is truly what Jesus came to do.

Practice the art of talking to strangers. If you aren't used to it, give it a try. Start conversations with statements. Have no other agenda except to connect, and you'll be amazed at how much you can learn and how much more open you'll become as "new perspectives" come pouring out of people.

If new perspectives make you feel threatened, you are not alone. This practice will challenge you, but you will come away with your truest beliefs not only intact but much stronger, and you won't get triggered and feel fear when someone challenges those beliefs.

Lastly, recognize and respect the inherent value in every person. Every person you meet is a soul that can be won to the Kingdom of God. Remember Paul's words, "From now on, therefore, we regard no one according to the flesh. Even though we once regarded Christ according to the flesh, we regard him thus no longer" (2 Cor 5:16 ESV).

CHAPTER ELEVEN:
Tell the Truth Even When It Hurts

To become more open to different perspectives, make a commitment. The commitment you need to make is to be a lover of the truth.

Why would loving the truth help you to be more open to new perspectives? Because if you make loving and learning the truth a higher value than proving your current beliefs right, then you have a much better chance of realizing when you have been wrong. Everyone hates being wrong, but that doesn't mean we shouldn't try to find the truth.

Let's take a look at a conversation between Jesus and the Pharisees to illustrate God's heart for the truth. In John 8, the author says,

> Again Jesus spoke to them, saying, "I am **the light of the world**. Whoever follows me will **not walk in darkness**, but will have the light of life." So the Pharisees said

to him, "You are **bearing witness** about yourself; your **testimony is not true**." Jesus answered, "Even if I **do bear witness** about myself, **my testimony is true**, for **I know** where I came from and where I am going, but **you do not know** where I come from or where I am going. **You judge according to the flesh;** I judge no one. Yet even **if I do judge, my judgment is true**, for it is not I alone who judge, but I and the Father who sent me. In your Law it is written that the **testimony** of two people is **true**. I am the one who bears witness about myself, and the Father who sent me **bears witness** about me." They said to him therefore, "Where is your Father?" Jesus answered, "You know neither me nor my Father. If you knew me, you would know my Father also." These words he spoke in the treasury, as he taught in the temple; but no one arrested him, because his hour had not yet come. (Jn 8:12–20 ESV emphasis added)

A little later, he says:

So Jesus said to the Jews who had believed him, "If you abide in my word, you are truly my disciples, and **you will know the truth**, and the **truth will set you free**." They answered him, "We are offspring of Abraham and have never been enslaved to anyone. How is it that you say, 'You will become free'?"

Jesus answered them, "**Truly, truly, I say** to you, everyone who practices sin is a slave to sin. The slave does not remain in the house forever; the son remains forever. So if the Son sets you free, you will be free indeed. I know that you are offspring of Abraham; yet you seek to kill me because **my word finds no place in you. I speak of what I have seen** with my Father, and you do what you have heard from your father."

They answered him, "Abraham is our father." Jesus said to them, "If you were Abraham's children, you would be doing the works Abraham did, but **now you seek to kill me, a man who has told you the truth** that I heard from God. This is not what Abraham did. You are doing the works your father did." They said to him, "We were not born of sexual immorality. We have one Father—even God." Jesus said to them, "If God were your Father, you would love me, for I came from God and I am here. I came not of my own accord, but he sent me. **Why do you not understand what I say? It is because you cannot bear to hear my word**. You are of your father the devil, and your will is to do your father's desires. He was a murderer from the beginning, and **does not stand in the truth, because there is no truth in him. When he lies, he speaks out of his own character, for he is a liar and the father of lies**. But because **I tell the truth**, you do not believe me. Which one of you convicts me of sin? If **I tell the truth, why do you not believe me?** Whoever is of God hears the words of God. The reason why you do not hear them is that you are not of God." (Jn 8:12–47 ESV emphasis added)

If you have ears to hear, this is a colossal statement about truth. I've highlighted the areas we'll look more closely at. Remember, our goal is to understand why we should be open to new perspectives.

Verse 12: "I am the light of the world." Jesus is telling us that he is the truth. He came to *illuminate*. Jesus is the *fact of reality* that illuminates and makes sense of every other fact of reality. Not only will he tell the truth, he *is* the truth. You and I can seek to be like him. That is, we can seek to know what is true, live our lives in a way that we could say we are truth, and go around speaking the truth.

"Whoever follows me will not walk in darkness." This is a powerful statement about the mindset of a true follower of Jesus. To fail to walk in the truth is to walk in darkness, to walk in *ignorance*. This is the very thing we must avoid. We must seek the truth, knowledge about the way the world actually is. This speaks to the powerful worldview we have, our understanding of the redemptive story of the whole race, the whole planet, that we find ourselves a part.

This will come up again, but Jesus is our example of "speaking the truth, even when it hurts." Remember, these words in John 8 were spoken to a hostile crowd, one that would indeed hurt him.

"You are bearing witness about yourself. Your testimony is not true" (v 13). The Pharisees accuse Jesus next of lying. They are looking to kill him for breaking the commandment to not bear false witness. This is exactly what happens in a good conversation where truth-telling is going on. Let's give the Pharisees the benefit of the doubt for now that they simply don't believe Jesus. One aspect of the truth-teller is that you are able to say in conversation, "I don't agree with you." This does not have to be done combatively. When people on one side or the other are making statements that hurt the cause of Christ because they are untrue, you don't have to be triggered, and you don't have to get into a huge argument. Remember, Jesus said we should not cast our "pearls before swine" (Mt 7:6). But you can always say, "I don't agree with you." If they truly want to know the truth, then they will engage honestly.

Sadly, the Pharisees were not actually interested in the truth. We see later in John 8 that they were arguing their side out of lies.

> You are of your father the devil, and your will is to do your father's desires. He was a murderer from the beginning, and **does not stand in the truth, because there is no truth in him. When he lies, he speaks out of his own character, for he is a liar and the father of lies.** (Jn 8:44 ESV emphasis added)

But for now, let's go back to earlier in the conversation. In verses 14–30, Jesus discusses where his truth comes from, the Father. We should ground ourselves in God's truth, so that when we speak the truth that hurts, we know where we "came from." We are not just speaking idly when we stand up for the truth. We are proclaiming the words of God. "I have **much to say about you and much to judge,** but **he who sent me is true,** and **I declare to the world what I have heard from him**" (v.26 emphasis added).

> As he was saying these things, many believed in him. So Jesus said to the Jews who had believed him, "If you abide in my word, you are truly my disciples, and **you will know the truth**, and the **truth will set you free**." (Jn 8:30–32 ESV emphasis added)

Why should we be willing to speak the truth, even when it hurts? Because the only way of setting people free is by the truth. Another reason is that things won't ever change unless we do.

Erroneous Thinking

Not too long ago, there were separate events that took place on two different mission trips I took that shared the same erroneous thinking. I was with a local mission team in the projects of my city. I was assigned to the food distribution team on that particular day. I noticed some of the fruit and vegetables had withered and started to grow mold. Horrified, I mentioned the condition of the perishable foods to the team captain who responded, "Don't worry about it. They should be happy to get anything we bring."

Thank God he didn't take that approach when he decided to send help for our sin problem. God sent his best. His one and only son, Jesus Christ. I had to then speak the truth and stand up for those we were serving. I finished my time and then didn't go back out with that organization.

A similar situation took place in Haiti with another group during a clothes distribution. I was sorting through the donations and removing the items that were really worn or soiled. One of the other members of the team approached me and said, "Look around, they will be glad to get anything we give them." Once again, human beings were being undervalued, and my soul was offended. These are the times when we must take courage and speak up, then be ready to back up our words.

I prayed about it first. I spoke to the missions pastor about some of the comments I heard, but he thought I was just being too sensitive. Then I began acting out what I thought God wanted to see from us as foreign missionaries in a country that desperately needed help. I lovingly addressed demeaning comments when I heard them. I also tried to demonstrate genuine compassion without judgment regardless of how people showed up for help.

This book is my attempt to "speak the truth." I want to start a conversation where it hasn't been started and continue it where it has. The way nothing will ever change is for all of us to be silent when the truth is burning in our hearts.

What Speaking the Truth Does for Us

We are committed to the truth primarily because Jesus calls us to it. God commands it. But there are no commands from God that are not grounded in causes. We don't have a faith that calls us to empty duty. There are grave consequences when we habitually lie or withhold what is true. The first consequence is that we lose self-trust when we come to know ourselves as someone who will not speak up. Self-trust may sound like something that is not important to a Christian. We think we are not supposed to trust ourselves, having been taught to think of ourselves as so bad that Jesus had to die for us. This is, of course, true, but it is a grave error to take that as a sign that we cannot do right. By the strength and Spirit of God we can do right. Consider how much ink is spilled in the Bible that is showing us the way to act and be. Is it there simply to show us how we *should be* if we weren't so depraved? I don't think so. Consider what James wrote:

> Know this, my beloved brothers: let every person be quick to hear, slow to speak, slow to anger; for the anger of man does not produce the righteousness of God. Therefore put away all filthiness and rampant wickedness and receive with meekness the implanted word, which is able to save your souls.

> But be doers of the word, and not hearers only, deceiving yourselves. For if anyone is a hearer of the word and not a doer, he is like a man who looks intently at his natural face in a mirror. For he looks at himself and goes away and at once forgets what he was like. But the one who looks into the perfect law, the law of liberty, and perseveres, being no hearer who forgets but a doer who acts, he will be blessed in his doing. (Ja 1:19–25 ESV)

It's clear from this passage that we are to be "doers of the word." If that is true, then one of the most important ways for us to "do the word" is by telling the truth, not lying, not withholding the truth we know in our hearts needs to be shared. As I previously stated, something awful happens to us when we are not honest. We're not trustworthy to ourselves or others. This is similar to when another person demonstrates their dishonesty to you. Now you cannot trust them. Anytime they say something, you will have to consider that they may be lying. It's the very same concept with ourselves. Gena Gorlin is a psychologist who has written extensively on the subject. In *Psychology Today,* she writes:

> Although self-deception is among psychology's most studied phenomena, the field doesn't even have a term for the opposite practice: deliberate self-honesty. Yet, as I've argued, this is among the most difficult and necessary character traits to cultivate if you're to live your own best life.
>
> Why? For one, because you can't make truly informed decisions if you distort or censor uncomfortable truths from yourself. If you selectively forget or rationalize away the mistakes you made on the last exam, you miss the chance to correct those mistakes on the next one. If you deny how unhappy you are in your work or relationship, you miss the chance to improve your lot, or even discover what improvements are possible. Just as you can't control the direction of your car if you don't keep your eyes on the road, so you can't control the direction of your life if you don't keep your eyes on reality.
>
> But there's another, related reason: **When we habitually avoid or distort reality, we lose credibility with ourselves**. If we routinely set intentions that part of us knows we won't keep, we eventually find ourselves struggling to take any of our intentions seriously. If we routinely talk ourselves into decisions that part of us knows

are unwise, we start doubting our judgment even when it's sound. *What if there's some lurking disaster I'm hiding from myself?* we wonder, whether in words or in the form of a vague anxiety. We don't trust ourselves to operate in reality, because we know our vision is compromised. As a result, we either stall out or defer to other people's judgment of what's best for us. Either way, we give up control. (Emphasis added)[13]

Confession

Gorlin's article is all about self-deception, which is the first step toward deceiving others. As Christians, however, we are called to be a people of the truth. We are called to come into the light. We invite God to shine a light on our hearts and show us "any offensive way" (Ps 139:24) in us. The spiritual discipline of *confession* has been given to us as a gift from God so that we can stop living a lie. 1 John 1:9 says, "If we confess our sins, he is faithful and just to forgive us our sins and to cleanse us from all unrighteousness" (ESV). And James 5:16 says, "Therefore, confess your sins to one another and pray for one another, that you may be healed. The prayer of a righteous person has great power as it is working" (ESV). Finally, Proverbs 28:13 says, "Whoever conceals his transgressions will not prosper, but he who confesses and forsakes them will obtain mercy" (ESV).

Most people live with dual identities. There is the person they show to the world, and there is the person they know themselves to be. Confession of sin is the first step toward

---

[13] Gena Gorlin, "5 Steps to Earning Your Own Trust," *Psychology Today,* August 5, 2020, accessed December 16, 2022. https://www.psychologytoday.com/us/blog/the-art-and-science-self-creation/202008/5-steps-earning-your-own-trust.

integrating those parts. According to Scripture, you will be forgiven of your sins if you confess them to God. But God invites us to confess to another brother or sister in Christ because when we do, he manifests himself in them. I come clean to the Christ in my brother or sister, and they can then speak a word of forgiveness and encouragement, which is God speaking. If we skip this step, we leave room for the evil one, the liar, to whisper routinely, "if anyone knew about this...." Well, God knows about it, and so does your friend, pastor, or whoever. Find someone you can trust and "confess your sins to one another and pray for one another, that you may be healed." After that crucial first step, be committed to ratting yourself out anytime you fall back or slip.

Speak the Truth in Love

Next, is to begin being honest about what you think. The Bible tells us to

> "speak the truth in love" (Eph 4:15 NLT)

to one another and to "put off falsehood and speak truthfully to your neighbor, for we are all members of one body" (Eph 4:26 NIV). Why speak the truth to one another? Because we are all members of one body. Just as it will ruin your life to lie to yourself, it will ruin the body, the community, the society to lie to one another because we are the same body.

People fail to speak the truth because they are afraid, but "perfect love drives out fear" (1 Jn 4:18 NIV). When you feel afraid to say what you think, ask God to help you to have love. You can ask him for courage, but it is love that you need, because the real love of Christ compels us (2 Cor 5:14 NIV) to do the hard things that must be done. Withholding the truth is easy to justify falsely using the word "love." But this is another deception. We say we love them, we don't want to hurt anyone's feelings. Have you ever looked inside a family and seen all the seething rage between the members? Everyone has opinions, but no one is willing to rock the boat, to upset whoever is the main source of the issues. Maybe your own family is like this.

The Church is a family, and things need to be said. Everyone needs to lovingly get their truth out on the table. By saying "their truth," I am not implying that truth is relative. I'm saying each of us has our own truths that we hold in our hearts and that we need to share, to bring into the conversation. Your truth could actually be wrong, an error. But it is still a truth to you because you honestly believe it. Part of the reason we need to start telling our truth is because we will never find out our errors if we don't.

Tell the truth, even when it hurts, because we belong to God and God is truth.

Conclusion

As I said in the very first paragraph, this book is intended to be a catalyst and the starting point of a conversation. The work itself is for you to do, for me to do, for our local congregations to do. There is still much to teach, to study, to discuss in our local churches and throughout the body of Christ. For some of us, this is our life's work. How will we know when our churches honor God's desire for diversity and inclusion? How will we know when there is true equity? How will we know when no one is being excluded based on differences and biases? The answer is the same one as that of the question, how do we know when we have been sanctified? This is a part of the work Christ started and left to us to continue until his return.

I hope that in Part One I made the case for God's heart for diversity, equity, and inclusion. The case is thoroughly biblical, and I hope I was able to give scriptural examples that help you in your prayer time, Bible study, and pastoral teaching. I also tried to show that love and unity are two subjects that are important to our Creator, and that he calls us to carry these in our heart as he does.

In Part Two, I outlined the COMMIT framework for making change in the areas of DEI, and I mused on how to go about it in our lives and our churches. I believe this book is a discipleship book as well, as everywhere I tried to be intentional about stating the main messages of the Gospel and the ministry of Christ and the Apostles. I believe that if you "COMMIT" to this work, it will change your life in more ways than just inviting diversity, equity, and inclusion. I believe it will make you more like the Son of God, our Lord and Savior, our Teacher, Jesus Christ.

This book is my calling, and I would put it the same way that Paul put his own calling to the Colossians:

> My goal is that they may be encouraged in heart and united in love, so that they may have the full riches of complete understanding, in order that they may know the mystery of God, namely, Christ, in whom are hidden all the treasures of wisdom and knowledge. (Col 2:2–4 NIV)

Making the effort to understand the mindset and specific actions needed to serve with a spirit of excellence is a matter of choice. Thankfully, The Apostle Paul gives us a clear blueprint to work from in 1 Corinthians 9:22–23:

> To the weak I became weak, to win the weak. I have become all things to all people so that by all possible means I might save some. I do all this for the sake of the gospel, that I may share in its blessings. (1 Cor 9:22 NIV)

The Message Bible puts it this way:

> Even though I am free of the demands and expectations of everyone, I have voluntarily become a servant to any and all in order to reach a wide range of people: religious, nonreligious, meticulous moralists, loose-living immoralists, the defeated, the demoralized—whoever. I didn't take on their way of life. I kept my bearings in Christ—but I entered their world and tried to experience things from their point of view. I've become just about every sort of servant there is in my attempts to lead those I meet into a God-saved life. I did all this because of the Message. I didn't just want to talk about it; I wanted to be in on it! (1 Cor 9:22)

I would like to close by leaving these summary thoughts:

1. **Christ above all**—Diversity, equity, and inclusion is not about "wokeness." They are, rather, additional ways of becoming more like Christ and fulfilling his mandate to make disciples of all nations. I do this work out of my

passion and reverence for Christ. Heaven is going to be the divine example of a diverse, equitable, and inclusive Church. It's time to bring some of God's sovereign design for the body of Christ in this world.

2. **God loves to take things that we don't understand and do something miraculous**— Do you think people understood the Messiah in a manger? Do you think the man born blind understood his high calling to glorify God (Jn 9:24)? Or did Abraham have any idea when God called him up to the mountain with his own son as the sacrifice, that, no, it would be God alone who would sacrifice his Son so that all others could be saved? God will do something miraculous, especially with those things we don't understand.

3. **We are God's plan for a time such as this**—If you find yourself praying that God would make the body of Christ more unified and that his Church would lead the way in the ministry of reconciliation across the globe, then it's a good prayer, just so long as we remember that we are also God's answer to our prayer. We help nonbelievers be reconciled to God and believers be reconciled to one another.

The ministry of reconciliation requires active participation from every believer.[14] One plants, one waters, and God gives the increase (1 Cor 3:7). As we proclaim the Gospel, we act as peacemakers and invite God's blessings (Mt 5:9). When

---

14 "What Is the Ministry of Reconciliation in 2 Corinthians 5:18?" *Gotquestions.org*, January 29, 2018, https://www.gotquestions.org/ministry-of-reconciliation.html.

we share and live out his message of reconciliation, lives are changed, and God gets the glory.

Allow me to leave you with a final, biblical Call to Action:

> In times of darkness, be the light. (Mt 5:14–16)
>
> In times of disinformation, be the truth. (Col 3:9–10) (3 Jn 1:4)
>
> In times of hate, be love. (1 Jn 4:20)
>
> In times of fear, be courageous. (Josh 1:9)
>
> In times of pain, be comfort. (2 Cor 1:4)
>
> In times of war, be peace. (Ro 12:18)
>
> In times of chaos, be still. (Ps 46:10)
>
> In times of uncertainty, be unmovable. (1 Cor 15:58)

We can respond to any situation with love and understanding without compromising our faith.

BIBLIOGRAPHY

Barkdull, Larry, "A Crucial Lesson from the Brother of the Prodigal Son." *Meridian Magazine*, January 28, 2019. https://latterdaysaintmag.com/a-crucial-lesson-from-the-brother-of-the-prodigal-son/

Bishop, Bill, and Robert G Cushing, *The Big Sort: Why the Clustering of Like-Minded America Is Tearing Us Apart* (Boston: Houghton Mifflin, 2008).

Bonhoeffer, Dietrich, *Life Together* (London: SCM Press Ltd., 1988)

Dei, Daniel, and Dennis E. Akawobsa, "Dietrich Bonhoeffer's Perspective on Racism," *HTS Teologiese Studies / Theological Studies* 78 (1) 2022: 7. https://doi.org/10.4102/hts.v78i1.7450

Erickson, Christine, "Biblical Justice & Social Justice," Shared Hope International, June 4, 2018. https://sharedhope.org/2018/06/04/biblical-justice-and-social-justice/.

Gorlin, Gena, "5 Steps to Earning Your Own Trust," *Psychology Today*, August 5, 2020, accessed December 16, 2022. https://www.psychologytoday.com/us/blog/the-art-and-science-self-creation/202008/5-steps-earning-your-own-trust

Hall, Christopher A., "The Habits of Highly Effective Bible Readers," *Christian History,* October 1, 2003. https://www.christianitytoday.com/history/issues/issue-80/habits-of-highly-effective-bible-readers.html.

Harris, La'Wana, *Diversity Beyond Lip Service: A Coaching Guide for Challenging Bias* (Oakland, CA: Berrett-Koehler Publishers, Inc., 2019).

Harris, La'Wana, *You Are Still Good: A Mother's Testimony of Faith and Prayer* (La'Wana Harris, 2017.)

Keohane, Joe, *The Power of Strangers: The Benefits of Connecting in a Suspicious World* (New York: Random House, 2021).

Keohane, Joe, "How to Become a Master at Talking to Strangers," *Entrepreneur,* July 7, 2021. https://www.entrepreneur.com/starting-a-business/how-to-become-a-master-at-talking-to-strangers/375641.

Lewis, Casey, "Christian Community Occurs in and through Jesus," *Christianity Matters,* November 19, 2013. https://christianitymatters.com/2013/11/19/christian-community-occurs-in-and-through-jesus/.

"Openness to Experience: Meaning, Examples & How to Improve Your Openness," HIGH5 TEST, accessed February 23, 2022. https://high5test.com/openness-to-experience/.

Strong's Greek Lexicon (mgnt), Blue Letter Bible, (n.d.). Retrieved July 5, 2022, from https://www.blueletterbible.org/lexicon/g4382/mgnt/mgnt/0-1/

"The 50 Countries Where It's Most Dangerous to Follow Jesus in 2021," *Christianity Today,* January 13, 2021. https://www.

christianitytoday.com/news/2021/january/christian-persecution-2021-countries-open-doors-watch-list.html.

"What Is the Ministry of Reconciliation in 2 Corinthians 5:18?" *Gotquestions.org.* January 29, 2018. https://www.gotquestions.org/ministry-of-reconciliation.html.